"SHOW ME!"

Devotions for Leaders to Teach Kids

by Susan L. Lingo

Group

Loveland, Colorado

DEDICATION

This book is dedicated with love to my brother Jim, whose room (and the strawberry pop!) were my first "show me" devotion on forgiveness. I love you, Jim.

"SHOW ME!" DEVOTIONS FOR LEADERS TO TEACH KIDS
Copyright © 1997 Susan L. Lingo

Visit our website: **group.com**

Credits

Editor: Lois Keffer
Managing Editor: Paul Woods
Chief Creative Officer: Joani Schultz
Copy Editor: Pamela Shoup
Designer and Art Director: Jean Bruns
Cover Art Director: Helen H. Lannis
Cover Designer: Richard Martin
Computer Graphic Artist: Randy Kady
Cover Photographer: Craig DeMartino
Illustrator: Shelley Dieterichs-Morrison
Production Manager: Ann Marie Gordon

Unless otherwise noted, Scriptures quoted from The Youth Bible, New Century Version, copyright © 1991 by Word Publishing, Dallas, Texas 75039. Used by permission.

Library of Congress Cataloging-in-Publication Data

Lingo, Susan L.
   "Show me!" : devotions for leaders to teach kids / Susan L.
   Lingo.
      p.   cm.
     ISBN 978-0-7644-2022-1
     1. Worship (Religious education) 2. Children—Prayer-books and
devotions—English. I. Title.
   BV1522.L56 1997
   242'.62—DC20
                            96–43493
                              CIP

26 25 24 23   17 16 15 14
Printed in the United States of America.

CONTENTS

DYNAMIC DUOS

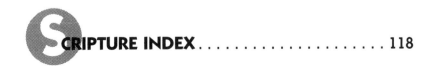

SCRIPTURE INDEX

INTRODUCTION

Everyone seems to offer devotions, but why? What's the big deal about devotions?

It's true that nearly every Christian education program offers a variety of devotions in addition to Bible stories and lessons. And there *is* a vast difference between stories, lessons, and devotions. Where stories and lessons teach about biblical circumstances, events, and people, devotions teach Christian values that are put into life practice. You can think of the difference as this: As lessons are to the mind, devotions are to the heart. A solid balance of biblical stories, lessons, and devotions rounds out Christian education. If any one element is missing, so is the fullness of God's Word!

So how is this devotional book different from others?

"Show Me!" Devotions for Leaders to Teach Kids is very different from the standard repertoire of children's devotions. These are devotions that *kids* learn to present. In all my classroom years as both a Christian and secular schoolteacher, the single most valuable teaching tool I've run across is . . . kids! Willing, ready, and motivated, peer-teachers often reach kids whom adults cannot. Yet some teachers, whether from vanity or a need to control, think children have no place as educators. Balderdash! Everyone has a lesson to teach as well as a lesson to learn, and children are no exception.

"Show Me!" Devotions is geared to teach kids to show other kids, who will show others, and so on and so on. What a great way to spread God's Word and build kids' self-esteem! And what a break for teachers! Seeing kids take responsibility for part of their learning is exciting and rewarding for teachers, kids, and parents. *"Show Me!" Devotions* offers kids not only snappy, eye-popping devotions, but the opportunity to serve others through teaching and sharing God's Word.

How do I use *"Show Me!" Devotions?*

Simply photocopy a devotion, and ask for a volunteer. I guarantee that after the first week, you'll have more volunteers than there are devotions! And you'll never tire of willing kids whose eyes shine as they share these devotions with classmates, friends, and family.

Each week, photocopy a devotion, choose a volunteer, and encourage the child to meet with you to practice the devotion or to practice it at home. That's it! You'll find these devotions to be simple, motivating, and big-time fun. And there are even devotions for pairs of kids to present, so the shy ones in your class won't feel pressured or left out.

As one teacher to another, I guarantee that after using these devotions, you'll never go back to the same old devotional format again! Kids CAN teach kids. Try it—you'll see!

Susan Lingo

TOTALLY
TERRIFIC
TRICKS

Eye of the Potato

GOAL GETTER:
Use raw potatoes to illustrate how Jesus wants us to share our possessions with others.

VERSE TO VIEW:
Matthew 19:24

TRICKS OF THE TRADE:
You'll need a Bible, drinking straws, and a raw potato for each child.

The Dynamite Devotion

Set out raw potatoes and drinking straws. Gather kids in a circle. Ask:
● **How hard do you think it would be for a camel to go through the hole in a needle?**

Hold up a potato and straw and ask:
● **How hard do you think it would be to make a straw go through a raw potato?**
● **Who thinks you can make a straw go through this potato?**

Choose a volunteer to make a few stabs at the potato. Then say: **It's not as easy as it looks, is it? It's even harder for a camel to go through the hole in a needle. And something else that's hard is sharing our things with others. It seems that having lots of money, time, toys, or clothes would make it easy to share with others. But Jesus taught that things aren't always as easy as they look. When we have a lot of something, we often forget to share. Jesus warned that it's hard to get to heaven if we forget to share, just as it's hard getting this straw into the potato. Let's see what the Bible tells us about being selfish with our possessions.**

Read aloud Matthew 19:24. Then say: **Jesus knows that selfish people have a hard time putting God first in their lives. But when we love God with all our hearts, it's easy to share with others!** Cover the top of the straw with your thumb, then thrust the straw firmly, at an angle, downward through the potato. The pressure from the air trapped inside the straw will strengthen the straw so it pierces the potato. **Sharing opens the gates of heaven and spreads God's love all around! Jesus is pleased when we share from our hearts.** Ask:

- When is a time you shared with someone?
- How did it feel to share? How did the other person react?
- Why is it important to share with other people?
- What is something you can share with someone this week?

Say: **Putting a straw through a raw potato is a good way to tell others about Jesus and how he wants us to share. Let's try the trick right now, then you can do this neat devotion at home for your family and friends.**

Toss raw potatoes and straws to the children, and explain the trick. Let them practice thrusting straws through the potatoes and explaining the concept of sharing to their friends. Let children take their potatoes and straws home. Encourage them to share their new trick with parents and friends and to tell how Jesus wants us to share with others.

Extra Excitement

- After everyone has tried the straw through the potato, peel the potatoes and cook up a pot of mashed potatoes to share. Or you may wish to serve potato chips and let kids take turns passing and sharing chips from the bag.
- Younger children will enjoy playing a game of Hot Potato. Play music and use a *real* potato to toss across the circle, having kids get rid of the potato as quickly as possible to avoid being stuck with it when the music stops.

TRICKY TIPS

✱ Choose a potato that's not too green. Also try this slick trick a few times so you're familiar with how to thrust the straw through the potato.

✱ Use the "straw through the potato trick" for finding the one true way to the Father through Jesus (John 14:6), and for knowing that everything is possible with Jesus (Philippians 4:13).

Choose Your Path

GOAL GETTER:
Use an arrow that switches direction right before their eyes to show kids the *right* path to God.

VERSE TO VIEW:
John 14:6

TRICKS OF THE TRADE:
You'll need a Bible, a clear drinking glass, water, an index card, a book, and a marker.

The Dynamite Devotion

Before class, fill a clear drinking glass with water. Be sure the glass is smooth and undecorated. Draw a thick, three-inch-long arrow, pointing to the left, across an index card, and write the word "evil" across the top of it. Set the glass of water on the table, and lay the index card next to the glass.

Gather kids and ask:

● **Who can tell about a time you were lost?**

● **How did it feel when you found the right way home or back to your parents?**

Say: **Did you know that sometimes we can become lost from God? Lots of things in the world are evil and try to draw us away from God. We become confused. We don't know which path to take.** Turn the arrow card so it continually changes directions. Then set the card on a table and prop it up with a book. Make sure the arrow is pointing to the left, then ask:

● **What kinds of things can turn us in the wrong direction?** (Lead kids to mention things such as doing drugs, listening to certain kinds of music, following friends who want to do bad things, telling lies, cheating, and disobeying parents.)

● **How can we stay on the right path to God?** (Lead kids to mention things such as reading the Bible, learning about God, and following Jesus.)

Say: **The Bible tells us a sure-fire way to stay on the right path to God. Let's read what it says.** Read aloud John 14:6. Then hold up the glass of water and say: **Following Jesus is the only way to stay on the right path to God. The Bible also tells us that Jesus is the living water—pure and life-giving. When we keep Jesus before us as our leader** (set the glass of water about five inches in front of the arrow), **we stay on the *right* path to God.** Let children peek through the glass of water at the card. The arrow should have switched directions and will now be pointing to the right. The word "evil" should now read "live"!

Say: **This is a pretty amazing trick, but following Jesus isn't a trick—it's the truth! In fact, Jesus is the only true way to God!**

Demonstrate the trick once more, and allow the children to try it. Encourage the children to perform this devotion for family and friends. Remind children to tell people that Jesus is the right way to God.

Extra Excitement

● Let your kids have fun making pathways across and around the classroom. Give each child a twenty-foot length of yarn or string to lay a personal path around the floor, making sure all yarn or string ends start at the same end of the room. Instruct kids to wind up the yarn or string as they go, taking care not to disrupt someone else's "path." Older kids will enjoy the extra challenge of being timed. Repeat the activity and see if kids can "wind" down the paths in less time.

● Kids of all ages love marble painting. Collect a variety of box lids and aluminum pie and cake pans. Lay a sheet of paper in each container. Set out small containers of tempera paint, and let kids drop marbles into the paint, then use plastic spoons to remove the paint-coated marbles and drop them onto their papers. Have children tip the containers back and forth so the marbles make paths of paint. Using a variety of colors makes a great design.

TRICKY TIPS

✳ Be sure to use a clear drinking glass with no patterns or raised designs.

Obedience Bottle

GOAL GETTER:

This amazing trick teaches kids that it's important to obey God in everything we do.

VERSE TO VIEW:

John 14:15

TRICKS OF THE TRADE:

You'll need a Bible; water; a plastic eyedropper; a drinking glass; and a clear, plastic liquid-detergent bottle. (You can find plastic eyedroppers at most pharmacies.)

The Dynamite Devotion

You'll need to prepare the obedience bottle before presenting this devotion. Be sure the empty detergent bottle is made of clear plastic and that you've rinsed out any remaining soap. Fill the plastic bottle almost to the top with water. Now fill a drinking glass with water. Place the empty eyedropper in the glass to see if it floats. Draw water into the eyedropper by squeezing the rubber bulb. If the dropper still floats, draw more water inside. Continue adding or taking away water until the bulb end of the dropper barely shows above the surface of the water.

Hold your finger over the open end of the eyedropper, and transfer it to the plastic bottle. Fill the bottle to the top with water. Make sure no air bubbles remain in the bottle, and screw on the bottle top. Squeeze and release the bottle. If you assembled your obedience bottle correctly, the eyedropper will plunge when you squeeze the bottle and rise when you release it.

Now you're ready to begin! Place the Bible and obedience bottle on a table, and gather kids around. Hold the side of the bottle with one hand and say: **Have you ever played a game with a bottle? It probably sounds impossible, but I'm going to play a quick game of Simon Says with this special obedience bottle and the eyedropper inside.** Play a game of Simon Says with the bottle, and give orders such as "Sit on the bottom, eyedropper" and "Hop to the top!" Slightly squeeze and release the bottle to make the eyedropper "obey" your commands. Try not to let your audience notice you squeezing the bottle.

After you've given several commands, tell the eyedropper to "sit," then release the bottle and ask:

● **What was the eyedropper doing in this trick?** (Lead kids to tell that the dropper was "obeying" your commands.)

● **Do you think it's important to obey "Simon" in a game? to obey God in our lives? Explain.**

● **What happens when we choose not to obey God?**

Say: **The Bible tells us lots of stories about people who chose to obey God and about those who didn't.** Read aloud John 14:15. Then ask:

● **How can you make sure to obey God this week?**

Say: **God wants us to obey him because he loves us and knows what's best for us. This tricky little eyedropper seemed to obey my commands, but we know it was just a cool trick. Obeying God isn't just a trick—it's the way to live!**

Demonstrate the trick once more and explain how you prepared the obedience bottle. Encourage kids to make their own obedience bottles and perform this devotion for family and friends. Remind children to tell people that we need to obey God in everything we do and say.

Extra Excitement

● Younger kids always enjoy a rousing game of Simon Says. Give this old game a new twist by choosing two leaders and having kids try to obey them both. Talk about how God is the only one we want to obey even if others are giving us orders.

● Form groups of three and encourage kids to brainstorm five important rules such as "no stealing" or "don't talk back to your parents." Then have each group explain to the class why it's important to obey these rules. Compare and contrast man's rules and God's rules. Point out that God's rules are meant to keep us safe and in line with God's will.

TRICKY TIPS

✳ If the eyedropper isn't "obeying," prepare the obedience bottle again from scratch. Be sure no water escapes the eyedropper as it's transferred from the glass to the bottle, and be sure no air bubbles remain in the bottle.

The Great Upside-Down Water Trick

The Dynamite Devotion

Fill a pitcher half full of water, and set it on the table with the sheet of stiff paper and the clear drinking glass. Gather kids around the table and ask:

● **What's a big problem you've faced? How did you solve it?**

● **Who do you turn to for help when you have big troubles?**

Say: **We all face many problems in our lives. Some of those problems seem small.** Pour a bit of water into the glass. **And some problems may feel too big to handle alone.** Pour more water into the glass until it's about three-quarters full. **Problems can turn us upside down!** Place the sheet of stiff paper tightly over the rim of the glass, then quickly turn the glass over and place it on the table upside-down. Hold the glass tight against the table and carefully slide out the sheet of paper. Voilà! You have an upside-down glass of water!

Look at the upside-down glass of water and say: **Now *this* is an interesting problem! Before we try to solve it, let's read what the Bible says about solving problems.** Have a volunteer read aloud Daniel 2:20-22. Then ask:

● **Who can solve all of our problems?**

● **Is there any problem God can't solve?**

● **How can we ask God's help with our problems?**

Say: **Now let's brainstorm ways to solve the problem of how to get the glass of water off the table.** Encourage kids to suggest solutions. Then hold the pitcher under the edge of the table. Hold the glass firmly against the table. Slide the glass to the edge of the table, and quickly empty the water into the pitcher. Say: **That wasn't so hard, was it? Remember, no problem is ever too big for God to solve.**

Demonstrate the trick once more and allow the children to try it. Encourage the children to perform this devotion for family and friends and to tell people that no problem is too big for God to handle.

Extra Excitement

● Have a little fun with creative problem solving. Form two groups and designate one group the Problem Posers and the other group the Super Solvers. Let the Problem Posers brainstorm one or two problems for the Super Solvers to creatively resolve. Suggest problems such as "How can a person travel to Antarctica?" or "What can someone do with his or her spare time?" If there's time, switch roles. Then talk about Bible stories that demonstrate God's ability to solve problems. You might mention the parting of the Red Sea, the supply of manna and quail in the wilderness, or the walls of Jericho tumbling down.

● Kids will have a blast painting "upside-down" pictures. Remove furniture along one wall. To protect the floor and wall from paint, tape newspapers along the floor and three feet up the wall. Tape sheets of newsprint (over the newspaper) on the wall about a foot from the floor. Now invite kids to "turn upside down" by spreading their legs and looking through them as they paint watercolor pictures!

TRICKY TIPS

✳ Keep a roll of paper towels on hand for quick spill-removal.

✳ Make sure the table has no dents, ripples, or cracked spots. The table surface must be perfectly smooth for this trick to work well.

Real A-Peel

GOAL GETTER:

Bananas bring home the point in this "a-peel-ing" devotion about God's good fruit.

VERSES TO VIEW:

Matthew 7:17-20

TRICKS OF THE TRADE:

You'll need a Bible, toothpicks, and a banana for each child in class plus one extra. Choose bananas that aren't overly ripe, but have a few brown speckles and spots.

The Dynamite Devotion

Just before devotion time, stick a toothpick through the ridge of the extra banana. Hold the banana vertically, and slide the toothpick gently back and forth in a straight line to slice the fruit horizontally inside the peel, making sure the toothpick doesn't exit the other side. Carefully withdraw the toothpick and repeat this process at one-inch intervals down the length of the banana. This banana will be the "bad" fruit.

Gather the children in a group, and hold up a banana. Say: **Jesus taught us that we're like fruit trees. If we're like good trees, we'll produce good fruit and treat others with kindness, forgiveness, love, and patience. But bad trees produce bad fruit. They're mean to others and say nasty things about them.** Ask:

● **What's it like when someone treats you in a mean way? How does it make you feel?**

● **What happens to rotten fruit?**

Say: **Sometimes fruit may look good on the outside when it's really rotten on the inside.** Hold up a "bad" banana and a "good" banana. Say: **I have some fruit here, but I can't tell which is good and which is bad. Maybe you can help.**

Hand one child the "bad" banana, and another child the "good" banana. **Let's see which fruit is good and which isn't. Peel your fruits!** As the "bad" fruit is peeled, slices will fall on the floor or table.

Say: **Wow! I guess we know which fruit is good and which is bad! The bad fruit isn't good to share with anyone, is it? Jesus wants us to be good trees that grow good fruit to share with others. Let's see what the Bible says about being good trees that produce good fruit.**

Read aloud Matthew 7:17-20. Then ask:

● **What's some "good fruit" we can share with others?** (Encourage children to report qualities such as being loving, patient, kind, and forgiving.)

● **What's some good fruit you're already growing in your life?**

Say: **When we share good things like love, kindness, and forgiveness, others learn about Jesus. Now let's see if you can do this "fruity" trick, then we'll have a good fruit snack!**

Hand each child a banana, a napkin, and a toothpick. Share the secret of how to slice bananas before they're peeled, and let children try this trick. When you're finished, let children eat their banana slices. Encourage children to surprise their families and friends with this slick trick as they explain about being Jesus' good trees and how we can produce good fruit to share with others.

Extra Excitement

● Bring in an assortment of sliced fruits, pretzel sticks, and a bowl of flavored yogurt. Invite children to poke the fruit with the pretzel sticks, then dip the slices in yogurt before eating them. Talk about the different kinds of "good fruits" in our lives and why each is important.

● Play a game of Fruit Basket Upset. Have each person choose a fruit to be, then choose one person to be "It." Instruct the "fruits" to line up at one end of the room and have It stand in the center. When It calls out the name of a fruit, all children with that fruit name hop to the opposite end of the room. The first person tagged becomes the next It. If It calls out, "Fruit basket upset," all the children hop to the other side of the room.

TRICKY TIPS

✳ Choose bananas that have small brown spots to camouflage the holes made by the toothpick. Overly ripe bananas will squish, while very green bananas won't slice easily.

✳ Use this slick banana trick to illustrate the way God sees what we're like on the inside (1 Samuel 16:7) and for finding out what's in a person's heart (Luke 6:45).

GOAL GETTER:
This dynamite devotion teaches kids that when we're weak, Christ is strong.

VERSES TO VIEW:
2 Corinthians 12:9-10

TRICKS OF THE TRADE:
You'll need a Bible, balloons, a black permanent marker, straight pins, transparent tape, and a paper towel with one end dipped in vegetable oil.

Pop Goes the Weakness!

The Dynamite Devotion

Before class, blow up and tie off two balloons. Draw a smiley face on one balloon and a sad face on the other. Now here is the key to this slick trick: stick one two-inch piece of transparent tape to the side of the happy-face balloon. Be sure the tape is stuck tightly to the balloon!

Place the balloons, the paper towel with vegetable oil, and a straight pin on a table. Hold up the sad-face balloon. Say: **I'd like you to meet Mr. Worried N. Weak. Mr. Worried N. Weak has a lot of troubles, and he's sure no one can help.** Ask:

● **What are things that make you worried or weak?**

Hold up the straight pin. Say: **Let's pretend this pin represents all the things that make us feel weak with worry or fear or sadness. What do you think will happen to Mr. Worried N. Weak when troubles poke at him?** Let kids tell you that Mr. Worried N. Weak will pop, then hold the balloon away from your face and stick it with the pin. **Whammo! Mr. Worried N. Weak explodes in a jillion pieces—or at least feels like he's exploded. What Mr. Worried N. Weak needs is someone to help keep him strong and "unpoppable." Let's see if the Bible tells us who is strong when we're weak.**

Read aloud 2 Corinthians 12:9-10. Then ask:

● **Who's our strength?**

● **How can we stay strong when we feel weak or fearful or worried?**

Say: **When we allow Jesus to carry our troubles, we become strong instead of weak—and troubles can't make us explode.** Wipe the pin with vegetable oil. Then hold up the happy-face balloon and gently push the pin through the center of the tape. The balloon will not explode. Say: **Voilà! When we give our weaknesses to Jesus, we're unpoppable and unstoppable! See how happy Mr. Worried N. Weak is now? But I think he needs a new name.** Let younger kids suggest names for the happy balloon.

Demonstrate the trick once more using a new balloon, then explain how it works. If you have time, allow the children to try it. Remind children to use tape on the balloon to keep it from popping. Then encourage the children to perform this devotion for family and friends and to tell people that when we're weak, Jesus makes us strong.

Extra Excitement

● Let children play a balloon juggling game to remind them of Christ's strength. Form groups of four or five, and give each group a balloon. Let groups begin batting the balloon back and forth to each other, naming a thing that makes them afraid, worried, or sad, such as storms, tests in school, or being sick. After a minute, hand each group a second balloon to keep in play. Continue adding balloons until the "worries" get to be too much and the balloons fall. Play again, only this time tell words that describe Jesus, such as "powerful," "strong," "loving," or "kind."

● Use tape, markers, balloons, colored construction paper, and drinking straws to make pretty balloon flowers to give to people who need a special "smile." Decorate balloons with colorful markers. Then tear paper leaves and tape them to drinking straws. Tape the straws to the knots in the balloons as stems. Include a card with each balloon flower that says, "Jesus' love makes us strong."

TRICKY TIPS

✳ If a balloon pops when stuck through the tape, it may have been a faulty balloon or the tape may have been loose. Blow up another balloon and try again.

✳ If you leave a pin stuck through the tape too long, it will pop. Gently remove the pin after the devotion, and throw the balloon away.

✳ Be sure to promptly discard any pieces of popped balloon.

GOAL GETTER:

This devotion about the healing power of Jesus will simply astound your audience.

VERSES TO VIEW:

Isaiah 61:1;
Psalm 34:18

TRICKS OF THE TRADE:

You'll need flat toothpicks, a man's handkerchief or a twelve-inch fabric square, and a Bible.

Mending Broken Hearts

The Dynamite Devotion

This devotion is especially well-suited for older kids to present. Before class, you'll need to prepare a special fabric square. Use a man's handkerchief with a one-quarter-inch hem, or sew a hem around a twelve-inch square of fabric. Carefully open a one-inch length of the hem on one side of the fabric. (See diagram below.) Slide a toothpick into this opening. Read through this devotion carefully and practice the trick several times to be sure you've got the hang of it. It's a really neat trick and well worth the practice time!

Before you begin, be sure you've hidden a flat toothpick in the hem of the handkerchief. Carefully hold onto the hidden toothpick during the devotion. Hold up another toothpick and say: **When we're born, our hearts are whole like this toothpick. But then things happen in our lives that make us sad or hurt inside.** Ask:

● **What are things that can break your heart or hurt your feelings?** (Lead kids to mention things such as lying, unkind words, or someone's sickness or death.)

Say: **All those hurts can break a heart for sure, just like we're going to break this toothpick.** Hold the flat toothpick

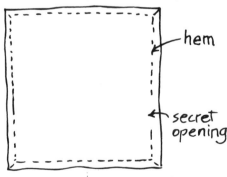

hem

secret opening

in your fingers, and cover your hand with the handkerchief. Now here's the tricky part: leaving the hidden toothpick in the hem, bring it up beside the whole toothpick under the cloth and drop the whole toothpick into your hand. When you've replaced the hidden toothpick in your fingers under the cloth, choose someone to come up and break the toothpick. (They're really breaking the *hidden* toothpick.)

Say: **Ouch! A broken heart can hurt. And we need someone who can fix a broken heart. But who can do**

that? Wait for kids to give suggestions. Then say: **Jesus is the only one who can mend a broken heart. Just like this.** Shake the cloth and catch the whole toothpick as it falls out of your other hand. The broken toothpick will remain in the hem. **It's not broken anymore! Jesus' love can heal wounds and mend broken hearts, just as this toothpick was mended. Let's read what the Bible tells us about how Jesus mends the brokenhearted.**

Read aloud Isaiah 61:1 and Psalm 34:18. Ask:

● **How does Jesus mend our hurt feelings and broken hearts?**

● **How can Jesus use other people to make us feel better?**

● **How can we go to Jesus with our deepest feelings?**

Say: **Remember, only Jesus can mend a broken heart, so when you're feeling sad, ask for Jesus' help.**

Demonstrate the trick once more as you explain how you prepared the hem in the fabric and slipped the toothpick inside. Encourage the children to perform this devotion for family and friends and to tell people that when we're hurt, Jesus can mend our hearts.

Extra Excitement

● Have kids sit in a big circle. Pass around a large paper heart, and as kids each tear off a piece, have them name a time their hearts were broken or their feelings hurt. Then pass out transparent tape, and have kids tape their paper heart pieces in place as they tell how Jesus helps mend broken hearts.

TRICKY TIPS

✽ Be sure to practice this trick before presenting it. The more you practice, the more smooth and amazing your presentation becomes!

✽ When you're done with the devotion, remove the broken toothpick, and immediately replace it with a new one. This way you'll be ready for your next "amazing performance" in a snap.

Simply Breathtaking

The Dynamite Devotion

Place the thumbtack, index card, and spool of thread on a table. Gather kids and ask:

● **What is "stick-to-itiveness"?**

● **What are some things worth sticking to?**

Say: **Some things are worth sticking to no matter what. Sticking to the truth is a good example. No matter how much we may be tempted to lie, it's always right to stick to the truth. The Bible tells us that Jesus is also worth sticking to. When we choose to stick to Jesus no matter what, it's called "commitment." Commitment is like a forever-promise from the heart. When we're committed to Jesus, we promise to love and follow him no matter who or what tries to push us away. It's great to be committed to Jesus, but it's not always easy.** Ask:

● **What kinds of things can push us away from Jesus?** (Lead kids to name things such as having bad friends, cheating, and saying mean words.)

Hold the index card to the bottom of the spool, and blow steadily through the hole in the spool. Let the card fall to the ground, then say: **Many things try to push us away from Jesus, just as this card was pushed away from the spool of thread. But *faith* helps us keep our commitment to Jesus.** Hold up the thumbtack, then stick it through the center of the index card as you say: **If we keep faith in the center of our thoughts and hearts, we stay committed to Jesus—and won't be pushed away.**

Take a deep breath, lean forward, and point the spool toward the ground. Steadily and firmly blow through the hole. At the same time, gently press the index card to the

blow air in here

other end of the spool. Stick the point of the thumbtack through the hole in the spool and hold it there a few seconds. If you're blowing firmly and steadily, you can remove your hand, and the card will stick to the spool!

Blow for a few more seconds, then put the spool and index card on the table. Say: **Just as the card stuck to the spool, we can stick to Jesus when we have faith. Faith helps us stay committed to following Jesus every day.**

Read aloud Psalm 37:5 and Proverbs 3:5-6. Then ask:

● **Why is it important to stick to Jesus?**

● **How can you stay committed to Jesus this week?**

Demonstrate the trick once more and explain that the thumbtack must stay in the center of the hole, and that it's important to blow firmly and steadily. If you have time, allow the children to try the trick a few times. Then encourage the children to perform this devotion for family and friends and to tell people that when we have faith, we stay committed to Jesus.

Extra Excitement

● Younger children will enjoy painting with empty spools. Let children dip the ends of various sizes and shapes of spools into tempera paint then stamp the ends on paper. Invite kids to try rolling the spools sideways in paint, then rolling "tracks" across their papers to create interesting designs. Point out how the paint sticks to the paper, just as we want to stick to Jesus.

● Give older kids a real challenge by having them form pairs and handing each child a craft stick or plastic spoon. Place several plates of rice or small noodles at one end of the room and empty bowls at the opposite end. Challenge pairs to link arms, then walk or hop to the rice, scoop some up, and transfer it to one of the empty bowls. Keep playing until all the rice or noodles have been transferred. Tell the kids that if any rice spills, they must pick it up. Talk about how committed kids were to their partners and to finishing the task. Then discuss how faith helps us keep our commitment to Jesus.

TRICKY TIPS

✳ Make up devotion totes for each child. For each tote, place a thumbtack, an index card, and a spool of thread inside a self-locking plastic bag. Distribute the totes at the close of class, and allow the kids to take their totes home after practicing the trick.

GOAL GETTER:

This devotion is a shining example of how Jesus takes our old lives and makes them fresh and new.

VERSE TO VIEW:

2 Corinthians 5:17

TRICKS OF THE TRADE:

You'll need tarnished pennies, paper towels, a container with two tablespoons of salt, a container with four tablespoons of lemon juice, baby food jars with lids, and a Bible. You'll also need a marker, tape, and two slips of paper. (If you plan to have the entire class do this activity, you'll need extra salt and lemon juice.)

The Old Becomes New

The Dynamite Devotion

Before this devotion, write the word "Forgiveness" on a slip of paper, then tape it to the container of salt. Write "Salvation" on another slip of paper, and tape it to the container of lemon juice.

Place a baby food jar, paper towel, and the containers of salt and lemon juice on a table. Hold up a tarnished penny. Ask:

● **Aren't pennies supposed to be shiny? What happened to this one?**

● **How is this tarnished penny like our lives when we do and say bad things?** (Lead kids to explain that things such as dishonesty, unkindness, and swearing make us "dirty" and tarnished like the penny.)

Drop the penny into the baby food jar, but don't put on the lid yet. Say: **Our lives are filled with things that make us dirty. We may become trapped in sin, and it makes us more and more tarnished. We soon have lives that are dirty and unclean. Help! We need someone to polish us and make us new—but that would be a pretty big miracle, right? In fact, is there anyone who can make us shiny and new again?** Pause for children to give their ideas.

Say: **Let's see what the Bible says about being made new and if there's even a way for that to happen.** Have a volunteer read aloud 2 Corinthians 5:17. Then ask:

● **Who's the only one who can make us new?**

● **How does Jesus make us new?**

Say: **Jesus is the only one who can give us new life. Jesus forgives the wrong things we do and say.** Hold up the container of "Forgiveness," then add the salt to the baby food jar. **And Jesus died for our sins and gives us his**

salvation. Hold up the container of "Salvation," then pour the lemon juice into the baby food jar. Place the lid on the jar, and begin to shake the contents. Pass around the jar, and allow each person to shake it for a few seconds. As the jar is being passed, talk about changes that occur in our lives when we become new through Jesus, such as how we begin to read the Bible, that we're kinder to everyone, that we become encouragers, and that we enjoy helping others.

When all the children have shaken the jar, remove the penny and wipe it with the paper towel. Hold up the shiny penny and say: **Just as this penny became like new, Jesus makes our lives like new. When we ask Jesus to take control of our lives, he gets rid of the yucky old stuff and makes us all shiny and clean!**

If you have time, explain how you prepared this trick. Encourage the children to perform this devotion for family and friends and to tell people that Jesus is the only one who can make our lives shiny and new. Give each child a shiny penny to take home.

Extra Excitement

● Play a game of Heads and Tails using shiny pennies. Have kids each find a partner and line up at one end of the room. Tell partners to choose who will be the Hopper and who will be the Flipper. Hand the Flippers each a shiny penny. When you say "go," have the Flippers flip the pennies. If the flip is heads, have the Hoppers hop ahead two times. If the flip is tails, have the Hoppers take one hop backward. When children reach the opposite wall, have Hoppers and Flippers switch roles.

TRICKY TIPS

✹ Use pennies that are moderately tarnished. Heavily tarnished pennies will shine, but will take much more "jar-shaking."

✹ You might wish to have all the children do this devotion at the same time as the person presenting the lesson. Allow kids to take their baby food jars and pennies home.

The Bodacious Balancing Act

The Dynamite Devotion

Hold the drinking glass on the palm of your hand. Say: **We're a lot like this fragile glass. If it tips or loses its balance, it will drop and shatter into lots of pieces. There are many things that can break our lives apart, too. What are some of those things?** (Lead kids to mention things such as a death in the family, a divorce, fights, and illness.)

Hold the glass beside the index card and ask:

● **What do you think will happen if I try to balance this glass on top of the card?** Pause for effect, then hold the card between your thumb and last three fingers as shown below. Carefully place the glass on the top edge of the card. Pretend to concentrate very hard on finding the point of balance. Then secretly slide your bent index finger up behind the card to support the bottom of the glass.

As kids "ooh" and "aah," say: **The only way we can keep a steady balance in our lives is through faith! Faith in Jesus' strength and love helps us through the hardest times and gives us balance so we don't fall and shatter apart.** Toss the glass slightly in the air and catch it.

Say: **Faith isn't something that we can see, but when it's inside us, we stay balanced. Let's read what the Bible says about having faith.** Read aloud Hebrews 11:1. Then ask:

● **How can having faith help you stay balanced?**

● **How can our faith get stronger?**

Say: **Remember, faith gives us a strong, steady foundation that will keep us from falling and breaking apart.**

Explain the trick, and demonstrate how to secretly

balance the glass with your index finger. Hand out index cards and paper cups. Allow the children to try this trick, then encourage them to perform the devotion for family and friends. Remind children to tell people that faith gives us a strong foundation for our lives.

Extra Excitement

● Place on the floor a variety of items to balance, such as pillows, tennis balls, paper cups, and cardboard boxes. Challenge kids to create their own balancing acts using one or more of the items. Talk about how difficult it is to remain steady as we try to balance more and more items. Remind kids that faith in Jesus keeps us steady every day of our lives.

● Use index cards to make card "castles." Point out how hard it is to find places to balance the cards and how when one card falls, many fall. Tell kids that faith always provides a sturdy, steady foundation on which to build our lives.

TRICKY TIPS

✱ Do this trick at the eye level of your audience so they can't see your index finger at work.

✱ Use a bit of water in the drinking glass for an even more daring balancing act!

Square Steppin'

1.

2.

3.

4.

5.

The Dynamite Devotion

Practice this trick several times before presenting it to your audience. You'll want to be comfortable with how to cut the index card, so follow the cutting directions carefully.

Place the Bible, scissors, and an index card on a table. Gather kids on the floor in front of the table, and say: **Let's see if you can do any of these simple tricks. First, give your elbow a kiss!** Pause for kids to attempt this trick. Then read the following directions and allow a few seconds for kids to try each one.

● **Balance on one finger for sixty seconds.**
● **Jump up and touch the sky.**
● **Scratch your back with your nose.**

Say: **Some things are impossible for people to do no matter how badly we want to do them.** Hold up the index card. Say: **Take, for instance, this little card. Who can step through it?** Pause for responses. Then say: **This trick seems totally impossible—even silly. Lots of things seem totally impossible, yet the Bible tells us there *is* someone who can do *all* things, no matter how hard or impossible they seem. Let's find out who that is.**

Have two volunteers read aloud Philippians 4:13 and Genesis 18:14. Ask:

● **Who does the Bible tell us can do anything?**
● **How does it make you feel to know that Jesus can do anything?**

Begin cutting the card according to the directions. As you cut, remind kids of Bible stories in which God accomplished things that would be impossible for people. You might mention the walls of Jericho falling down, the sun stopping in the sky, Jesus calming the storm, and the biggest impossibility of all—Christ's resurrection!

Continue cutting the card until you're ready to open it

up. Then say: **Many people in the Bible learned that with God's help, all things are possible. And it's important for us to realize it, too. When we ask for Jesus' help, we can do anything!** Open up the card, stretch it out, and invite each child to carefully step through as he or she says, "I can do anything through Jesus."

Say: **This is a cool trick, but knowing that Jesus can do anything isn't a trick at all—it's the truth! Be sure to show this great trick to your families and friends and tell them that nothing is impossible with Jesus!**

Give each child an index card and scissors. Demonstrate how to cut the card as kids follow along. Then hand each child a few more index cards and a copy of the cutting directions to take home. Encourage kids to do this devotion for family and friends and to tell people that with God, nothing is impossible.

Extra Excitement

● Older kids will enjoy the challenge of using the cutting directions on various sizes and types of paper. Use wrapping paper, construction paper, and comic pages from the newspaper. Then tape the colorful loops together and hang them around the room to remind everyone that nothing is impossible with Jesus.

● Cut a series of loops, and lay them on the floor around the room. Cut one loop for every three kids. Have kids stand in the loops. When you call out, "Nothing is impossible with Jesus," have the kids hop to find new loops to stand in. Tell kids to be sure they have at least one foot in a loop. Then remove one loop and play again. Continue until everyone has to fit one foot in the same loop.

TRICKY TIPS

✱ Practice cutting until you know how to cut the index cards without referring to the directions.

✱ Lay the card on a table when cutting the inside slits.

Up From the Tomb

GOAL GETTER: This simple but effective Easter devotion will help kids remember that Jesus conquered death because he loves us.

VERSE TO VIEW: John 15:13

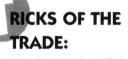

TRICKS OF THE TRADE: You'll need a Bible, a pack of playing cards in a box, and scissors.

The Dynamite Devotion

Before class, snip a one-quarter-inch-wide by two-inch-long slot in the center of the back of a box of playing cards. Find the three of hearts and place it at the back of the card box, then slide the rest of the cards into the box. Practice sliding the three of hearts out of the box by pushing the card up with your index finger. Be sure the card is facing your audience. Keep the three of hearts at the back of the card box all the time, and never show your audience the back of the box!

Gather kids on the floor in front of you. Hold the deck of playing cards, and say: **Put your hand on your heart if you remember the Easter story and how Jesus died on the cross.** Pause. Then say: **You can help me retell the story with these cards. When I say a number, help me count out the right number of cards.** Remove all the playing cards from the box except the three of hearts. Don't let your audience see the card in the box! Count out the correct number of cards as you tell the following story. Lay the cards face down on the floor as you count. Encourage your audience to count with you.

Jesus was God's ONE (count one card) **and only Son. He had come to teach people about God's love, but many people didn't believe Jesus or even like him. Jesus came to Jerusalem for the Passover feast, and ONE** (count one card) **evening, Jesus and his TWELVE** (count twelve cards) **disciples ate supper together. It was a special supper—and it would be Jesus' last supper on earth. Jesus and his disciples shared ONE** (count one card) **loaf of bread and ONE** (count one card) **cup of wine. Jesus told his disciples to eat and drink the bread and wine to remember his love.**

Then Jesus did something surprising. He washed the feet of his disciples to show them how to serve one another. Just think! Jesus washed TWENTY-FOUR feet! (Count twenty-four cards.) **Then Jesus told Peter that Peter would say he didn't know Jesus THREE times before the**

rooster crowed in the morning. (Count three cards and have kids crow as you count.)

Jesus took THREE (count three cards) **of the disciples to a beautiful garden to pray. But just as Jesus finished praying, mean soldiers arrested him. They took Jesus to the home of the high priest. Peter watched from far away. People asked Peter if he knew Jesus and THREE times Peter said he didn't.** (Count three cards, and have kids crow as you count.) **Then the people who didn't like Jesus wanted him dead. On that ONE day** (count one card), **they hung Jesus on a cross until he died. God's ONE** (count one card) **and only Son was dead, and Jesus' disciples felt sad and mixed up.** Shuffle the cards.

Then they put Jesus in a cold, dark tomb. Pick up the cards and place them in the card box. Be sure to place them *in front* of the three of hearts! Hold the box of cards, and place your index finger on the slot. Say: **But did Jesus stay dead? No! On the third day, Jesus rose from the tomb!** Push the three of hearts up. **Jesus conquered death because he loves us and wants us to live with him forever.**

Read aloud John 15:13, then ask:

- **What do you do to show that you love someone?**
- **What shows how much Jesus loves us?**

Demonstrate and explain how the trick works. If you have time, allow the children to try sliding the three of hearts up from the back of the box. Be sure to point out to children that the three of hearts must remain in the back of the card box at all times. Encourage the children to perform this devotion for family and friends and to tell people that Jesus rose from death because of his great love for us.

Extra Excitement

- Get an extra "rise" out of your kids by making Rise 'n' Shine Easter Rolls. Let kids put dabs of butter in the bottom of muffin cups, then sprinkle one tablespoon of brown sugar on the butter. Sprinkle a few chopped pecans on the brown sugar if desired. Then place a canned refrigerator biscuit in each muffin cup. Bake the rolls at 325 degrees until they're golden brown, then immediately turn over the muffin pan on a cookie sheet to release the caramel rolls.

TRICKY TIPS

❋ Don't let anyone see the back of the card box as you're presenting the devotion.

❋ Practice telling the story in your own words. And remember, the number sequence is: 1-1-12-1-1-24-3-3-3-1-1-shuffle-return-raise.

GOAL GETTER:
This fascinating devotion teaches kids what witnessing is all about.

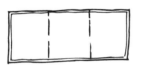

VERSES TO VIEW:
Matthew 28:19-20

TRICKS OF THE TRADE:
You'll need a Bible, paper clips, and dollar-bill-sized pieces of green paper. Be sure the paper clips are all the same size.

The Stupendous Paper Clip Hug

The Dynamite Devotion

Before class, cut out a dollar-bill-sized piece of green paper for each child in class. Practice folding the "dollar" in an S shape. Then carefully follow the diagram below to attach two paper clips to the dollar. Be sure you attach the paper clips with the *short* loops facing you. After the paper clips are attached, hold the ends of the dollar and pull, snapping them apart. If you folded the dollar and attached the paper clips correctly, the paper clips will link together as they fly into the air. Practice this trick a few times to get the hang of it!

Place the dollar and paper clips beside you. Ask the class:

● **When's a time you told an important message?**

● **What might have happened if you hadn't gotten the message through?**

Say: **There are times when it's really important to deliver a message. Maybe someone is sick, and you need to tell a doctor. Or maybe you'll be late to dinner, and you need to tell your mom so she won't worry. All those messages are important. But the Bible tells us about the most important message of all.**

Hold up the dollar. Say: **Jesus has a message for us that's like a precious treasure. And he wants us to tell that message to everyone we know.** Fold the dollar in an S shape. Attach the paper clips as you say: **When we tell someone that Jesus loved them enough to die for the wrong things they've done, we become linked to that person with Jesus' love!** Snap the dollar, and let the paper clips fly. Then hold up the linked paper clips. **See? It's like linking each other in a love-hug from Jesus!**

When we tell someone about Jesus' love, that person becomes linked to Jesus and can tell other people, too. That's what witnessing is all about.

Let's read what the Bible tells us about witnessing to others.

Have a volunteer read aloud Matthew 28:19-20. Then ask:

- **Who are we supposed to tell about Jesus?**
- **Why is it important to be witnesses for Jesus?**
- **Who is one person you can witness to this week?**

Say: **The paper clip hug is a great trick. But it's no trick when we tell others about Jesus!**

Distribute a paper dollar and two paper clips to each child. Carefully explain how to hold the paper and attach the paper clips. Encourage the children to perform this devotion for family and friends. Remind children that witnessing to others means telling them about Jesus and his love. Let children take their bills and paper clips home.

Extra Excitement

- Let children use markers or crayons to decorate their paper dollars. As they work, point out that telling others about Jesus is like giving them a great treasure that's worth more than all the money in the world.

- Clear an area in your room and play a game of Link Tag. Choose someone to be the Chain. Each time the Chain tags someone, that person must link elbows with the Chain and help him or her tag others. Instruct kids that the only rule is to hop or walk heel-to-toe during the game. Remind kids that telling others about Jesus links us together in love.

TRICKY TIPS

✳ Try using a real dollar bill for this devotion, then hand out photocopies for the children to take home.

✳ The key to this trick is in attaching the paper clips correctly. Be sure to follow the illustrated instructions.

The Secret Square

GOAL GETTER:

In this fantastic devotion, kids will realize the importance of contemplating God's Word.

VERSE TO VIEW:

Psalm 119:11

TRICKS OF THE TRADE:

You'll need a Bible, a dictionary, a paper lunch sack, paper, and pencils.

The Dynamite Devotion

Place a sheet of paper, the lunch sack, and nine pencils beside you. Set the dictionary and Bible on a table. Ask:

● **What's the most important word or words you know?**

● **Which book do you think has the most important words to learn and think about: the dictionary or the Bible? Why?**

Say: **We often use the dictionary to find important words. But did you know that the most important words of all are found in the Bible? In fact, the Bible is often called "God's Word." And God's Word is so important that he tells us to learn and think about it all the time.** Ask:

● **What are some important words found in the Bible?** (Lead kids to suggest words such as hope, faith, love, forgiveness, and Jesus.) Then say: **Let's write down some important words from the Bible. First we need slips of paper.** Tear the sheet of paper into nine small rectangles. (See diagram below.) The center rectangle will have four rough edges.

Choose nine volunteers to come forward, and hand each person a rectangle of paper and a pencil. Remember which child gets the rectangle with four rough edges. Instruct the kids to each write a word from the Bible on their papers, then drop the papers into the lunch sack.

Say: **Now I'll read the words aloud and tell which one of you wrote a certain word.** Pause for a moment, then say: (Name of person who had the rectangle with four rough edges), **I think I'll identify your word.** Reach into the sack and pull out the slips of paper. Read aloud each word, saving the paper with the rough edges for last.

Then identify the person who wrote the word on the paper with four rough edges. Be prepared for surprised kids to ask, "How did you know that?"

Say: **When we learn and think about God's Word, we know how to do what it says. Let's see what the Bible says about thinking about God's Word.** Have a volunteer read aloud Psalm 119:11. Then ask:

● **Why is it important to learn and think about God's Word?**

● **How does learning God's Word help you?**

● **What's one word from the Bible you can think about this week?**

Explain the trick, and demonstrate how to tear the rectangles. If you have time, allow the children to get into pairs and try the trick. Then encourage the children to perform this devotion for family and friends and to tell people that it's important to learn, think about, and apply God's Word in their lives.

Extra Excitement

● Have older kids make a list of Bible words, such as love, faith, hope, forgiveness, mercy, grace, and obedience. Then let pairs of kids look up the words in a regular dictionary and in a Bible dictionary. Compare and contrast the meanings of the words. Then have each pair tell ways they can put those words to work in their lives.

● Let younger kids glue uncooked alphabet pasta or alphabet cereal letters to paper plates to make words from the Bible. Consider having them spell out the phrase: "God is love." Let them color the edges of the paper plates with markers or crayons.

TRICKY TIPS

✳ Do your best to tear the paper into rectangles of the same size.

✳ Thin copy paper or notebook paper work best for this trick.

It's in the Bag

OAL GETTER:
This slick trick will teach kids that God's Word can't be destroyed—it's made to last forever!

ERSE TO VIEW:
Isaiah 40:8

RICKS OF THE TRADE:
You'll need a Bible, paper lunch sacks, paper, pencils, scissors, and transparent tape.

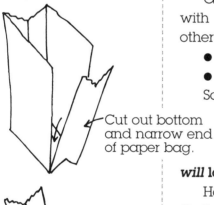

Cut out bottom and narrow end of paper bag.

narrow end and bottom

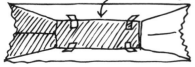

Tape edges of bottom along inside bottom of new bag.

The Dynamite Devotion

Before this devotion, cut out the bottom and one narrow side of a paper lunch sack. Cut out the bottom and side in one piece as shown in the diagram below. Now place the bottom of the cut piece along the inside bottom of another identical bag, matching the edges carefully. You want it to appear as if this inserted piece is really the bottom of the new bag. Tape the edges of the bottom piece securely to the bag so the side piece folds back and forth like a flap. This will be the "secret hiding place" during your trick! Now write Isaiah 40:8 on **two** heart-shaped pieces of paper. Hide one of the hearts behind the flap in your secret hiding place.

Gather kids in front of you on the floor. Place the bag with the hidden heart in your lap and the Bible and other paper heart beside you. Ask:

- **How long is forever?**
- **What's something that lasts forever?**

Say: **It's hard to think of something that lasts forever. Living things die, and even huge rocks break down into bits of sand and soil that are washed away. But the Bible tells us about one thing that** *will* **last forever. Let's find out what it is.**

Have a volunteer read aloud Isaiah 40:8. Then say: **God's Word truly lasts forever.** Hold up the paper heart and read the verse on it. Now begin to tear the heart into small pieces. **God's Word lasts forever because it's true— and God's truth never changes. I have an empty bag that we can pretend is like our hearts.** Hold the loose side of the bag to keep the paper heart from sliding out, and quickly show kids the inside of the bag. **When we learn God's truth and hide it in our hearts, it stays safe and sound.** Carefully place the torn pieces of the heart in the bag's secret hiding place. Shake the bag a few times for effect, then carefully reach inside the hiding place and pull out the whole paper heart. **See? God's Word stays safe and sound and complete—it can't be destroyed!** Hold the flap against the side of the bag, and quickly show kids the "empty" insides.

Explain the trick, and demonstrate how it works. Hand out paper lunch sacks, tape, scissors, sheets of paper, and pencils. Let children make paper hearts then get into pairs to try this trick. Encourage kids to perform the devotion for family and friends and to explain that God's Word can never be destroyed because his Word is the everlasting truth.

Extra Excitement

● Give older kids practice using a concordance by playing a game of Scripture Search. Be sure that everyone knows how to use the concordances in the back of their Bibles, then have kids get into pairs or trios. Give each small group one of the following references to look up or have everyone search for the same verse simultaneously. Then allow kids to take turns reading the verses aloud and telling why each verse is important. Look up Romans 3:23; Ephesians 2:8-9; John 3:16; Philippians 4:13; and Psalm 100:3 or add more of your own choosing.

● Provide markers, crayons, glitter pens, and stickers. Invite kids to get creative and decorate their paper lunch sacks with the words, "God's Word Lasts Forever!" Older kids might want to write Isaiah 40:8 on their bags.

TRICKY TIPS

✳ Practice making scraps of paper "disappear" and the whole heart "reappear" before presenting this devotion. The more smoothly you're able to hide "God's Word," the more amazing your trick will seem.

Lift Your Hearts

GOAL GETTER:

This devotion will "lift" kids' hearts as they learn that Jesus carries our troubles and helps us.

VERSES TO VIEW:

Matthew 11:28-30

TRICKS OF THE TRADE:

You'll need a Bible, water, a clear jar, a red permanent marker, table salt, a spoon, and hard-boiled eggs. Write "JESUS" on the side of a paper cup, then pour one-half cup of salt into the paper cup.

The Dynamite Devotion

Before class, use a red permanent marker to draw a red heart on a hard-boiled egg. Be sure the marker is permanent or the heart will wash away during the devotion.

Fill a clear jar half full of water. Place the jar of water, a spoon, the box of salt, and the hard-boiled egg on a table. Gather kids in front of the table. Hold the hard-boiled egg so kids can see the heart. Say: **Sometimes our hearts feel heavy with worries or fears. What's one fear or worry you've had?** Allow time for responses.

Say: **When our hearts become full of worries and fears, they seem to sink inside us.** Drop the egg into the jar of water. **Ugh! Nothing feels as bad as a sunken heart! But *how* can we feel good again? Who can take away our worries and fears and make our hearts light? Jesus can!** Pour the salt into the jar. As you stir the water, say: **Let's see what the Bible says about Jesus lifting our hearts.**

Have a volunteer read aloud Matthew 11:28-30. Continue stirring the water, and say: **Jesus wants us to give him our worries and fears. He doesn't want our hearts to feel heavy because he wants to fill us with joy.** When the egg rises to the top and floats, say: **When we give our worries and fears to Jesus, our hearts become lighter!** Stop stirring and let the kids peek at the floating "heart." Then ask:

● **What's one worry or fear you can give Jesus this week?**

Say: **Remember, when we give our heavy troubles to Jesus, he lightens our loads.**

Hand each child a hard-boiled egg, then explain how to do the trick. Be sure kids understand that they'll need to use one-half cup of salt to make the egg rise in the water. Encourage kids to perform this great devotion for family and friends and to explain that when we give our heavy troubles to Jesus, he lightens our loads.

Extra Excitement

● Make additional hard-boiled eggs and let kids prepare egg salad for a special treat. Have kids peel the eggs and use plastic knives to cut them into small pieces. Help them mix the diced eggs with mayonnaise and a bit of salt and prepared mustard. Invite kids to spread egg salad on crackers and enjoy a "light" snack.

● Invite older kids to decorate unpeeled hard-boiled eggs with colorful permanent markers. Encourage them to incorporate heart shapes into their designs. Remind kids to keep the ink on the eggs—not on their clothes!

TRICKY TIPS

✳ The water may appear slightly cloudy as the salt dissolves, but kids should still be able to see the "light-hearted" floating egg.

The Amazing Water to Wine Trick

OAL GETTER:
This eye-popping trick teaches kids about Jesus' miracles—and that he can do anything.

ERSE TO VIEW:
Mark 9:23

RICKS OF THE TRADE:
You'll need a Bible, unsweetened grape juice, water, baking soda, three clear drinking glasses, a spoon, white vinegar, and measuring cups and spoons.

Grape Juice | VINEGAR

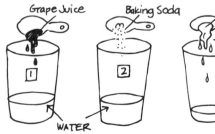

Grape Juice | Baking Soda | Vinegar

1 | 2

WATER

The Dynamite Devotion

Before this devotion, set the three drinking glasses on a table. Pour one-quarter cup of water into the first and second glasses. Measure carefully so your trick will work! Add one teaspoon of baking soda to the second glass of water. Mix well to dissolve the baking soda. Pour two tablespoons of white vinegar into the third glass. Then add one tablespoon of grape juice to the first glass to make the water a light purplish-red color. Now you're ready for some fun!

Gather kids in front of the table so they can see the three glasses. Ask:

● **What's the most amazing thing you've ever seen or heard of?**

● **Could you believe it? Why or why not?**

Say: **The Bible is full of stories about wondrous events and happenings—some are almost too amazing to believe. But because the Bible is God's Word, we know the stories are true. We call these wondrous happenings "miracles." Let me tell you about Jesus' first miracle.**

Jesus, his mother Mary, and some of his friends went to a wedding party in the town of Cana. (KAY-nuh) Hold up the first glass containing grape juice. **The people at the party ate delicious foods and drank wine until it was all gone.** Slowly pour the liquid from the first glass into the second glass. **There was no more wine anywhere—there was only well water. Mary felt sorry for her friends who were hosting the party and couldn't give their**

guests more refreshments. So Mary quietly asked Jesus for help. Mary knew that Jesus can do anything.

Jesus asked a servant to bring jars of water from the well. Then guess what Jesus did? Jesus turned the water to wine! Slowly pour the liquid from the second glass into the third glass. The liquid will turn red. **Jesus turned water to wine to help his friends. And that was Jesus' first miracle.** Read aloud Mark 9:23, then ask:

- **Why do you think Jesus performed miracles?**
- **How can Jesus' power help us today?**

Say: **It looked like I turned wine to water and water to wine, but it was only a neat trick. Jesus' miracles are real because Jesus can do anything. It's important to know that miracles come from the Lord and that his power can help us any time, any place.**

Explain the trick, and demonstrate how it works. Tell kids how much water, baking soda, grape juice, and vinegar to use in the drinking glasses. You may want to photocopy instructions for each child. Then encourage kids to perform this incredible devotion for family and friends. Remind kids to explain that only the Lord can do miracles, and we can rely on him to help us in amazing ways.

Extra Excitement

- Let kids use crayons to color pictures of their favorite miracles from the Bible. Then provide bowls of grape juice and paintbrushes or cotton swabs and let them paint over the crayon to make an unusual "crayon-grape juice resist" picture. Display the works of art in a hallway "gallery" titled "Miracles Made in Heaven."

- Young children love playing the game Can You Do This? Form a circle, and choose one child to say, "Can you do this?" Then have the child perform a trick, such as standing on one foot, patting his or her head, and whistling a tune all at the same time. Have the other kids imitate the trick if they're able to, then choose another person to lead a trick. When you're through playing, remind children that only Jesus can do *everything*.

TRICKY TIPS

✱ Be sure to measure the grape juice, baking soda, water, and vinegar accurately.

✱ For the best results, use clear eight-ounce drinking glasses.

Boiling Over With Joy

GOAL GETTER:

This clever devotion will have kids "bubbling" over with surprise as they recognize the Holy Spirit as our special helper.

VERSES TO VIEW:

John 14:16-17

TRICKS OF THE TRADE:

You'll need a Bible, clear drinking glasses, paper plates, rubber bands, cheesecloth, scissors, and water.

The Dynamite Devotion

Before presenting this devotion, cut six-inch squares of cheesecloth. You'll need two squares for each pair of kids plus two extra squares.

Just before the devotion, fill a glass with water. Place two cheesecloth squares over the top of the glass, and secure them with a rubber band. Wet the top of the cheesecloth by running your wet hand over the entire surface of the cloth. Place the cloth-covered glass, paper plate, and Bible on a table.

Gather kids in front of the table, and say: **I have an amazing trick to show you today. We'll make the water in this glass boil without any flames, fire, or stove.** Quickly turn the glass upside down over the paper plate. (A few drops of water may dribble out, but they should stop immediately.) Then lift the glass from the plate and call someone to come forward and push gently on the cheesecloth with his or her index finger. Hold the glass in one hand as you push the glass downward with your other hand. Bubbles will rise to the top of the water as if it's boiling! When the bubbles stop, set the glass upright on the paper plate.

Say: **Wow! Did you see that water bubble and boil? Yet there seemed to be no heat powering it. You know, this is a lot like how the Holy Spirit works in our lives. Jesus sent the Holy Spirit to be our special helper and empower us to do mighty things to bring honor to God. Even when we can't see the Holy Spirit at work, we can trust he's there helping us! Let's see what the Bible tells us about the Holy Spirit.**

Have a volunteer read aloud John 14:16-17. Then ask:

● **What sorts of things do you think the Holy Spirit does in our lives?**

● **How can we know that the Holy Spirit is at work even when we can't see him with our eyes?**

● **How can you let the Holy Spirit "fire you up" to help others this week?**

Say: **Just as this water bubbled and boiled without a flame, the Holy Spirit "fires us up" to help others and do mighty things for God.**

Explain the trick and demonstrate how it works. Have kids get into pairs and try the trick with fresh pieces of cheesecloth. Encourage kids to perform this incredible devotion for family and friends. Remind kids to explain that only the Lord can do miracles, and we can rely on him to help us in amazing ways.

Extra Excitement

● Make unique, sparkly sculptures by mixing glitter, white craft glue, and water in a shallow bowl. Give each child a twelve-inch square of cheesecloth, a sheet of aluminum foil or wax paper, and a paper cup. Show kids how to dip their cheesecloth in the glue mixture, wring out the excess liquid, then drape the cloths over paper cups to form sculptures. Demonstrate how to pinch the edges or make wavy ruffles in the cloth. When kids have created the shapes they want, allow the cloths to dry for a few days. The cloths will stiffen creating unusual sculptures.

TRICKY TIPS

✳ Be sure to wet the cheesecloth thoroughly before turning the drinking glass upside down.

✳ If you can't find cheesecloth, a man's handkerchief will work. If you use a handkerchief, you'll need only one layer of cloth to cover the drinking glass.

The Tricky Pick-Me-Up

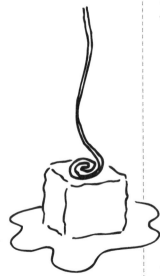

The Dynamite Devotion

Before class, cut a ten-inch length of string or yarn for each child in class. Be sure you have an ice cube and a paper plate for everyone.

Wet the ends of one string just before the devotion. Then place the salt, string, tape, and glue on a table. Set an ice cube on a paper plate. Say: **I have a dilemma. My goal is to find a way to pick up and stick close to this ice cube, but I'm not sure how to do it. There are lots of things here to use, but how do I know which ones will help and which won't? How do you think I should pick up the ice cube without using my fingers?**

Encourage kids to give their ideas. Then hold your index finger to your lips to silence the group. Quietly wind a few inches of the string on top of the ice cube. Pour about one-quarter teaspoon of salt on top of the string on the ice. Ask the kids to help you count to fifteen, then gently lift the end of the string. The ice cube will stick to the string and be lifted in the air.

Say: **See? All it takes is knowing what ingredients will help and what won't. The same thing is true when we want to stay close to Jesus. We need to know what helps us stick to him and what pushes us away.** Ask:

• **What helps us stick close to Jesus?** (Lead kids to mention things such as reading the Bible, praying, going to church, and being kind to others.)

• **What things push us away from Jesus?** Mention things such as lying, being mean to others, and disobeying God.

Have a volunteer read aloud Matthew 16:24. Then say: **Our goal is to stick close to Jesus. We just need to**

know what helps us do this, then we need to *do* it!

Explain the trick, and demonstrate how it works. Then have kids get into pairs. Give each pair two paper plates, two pieces of string, salt, and two ice cubes. Instruct the kids to rub an end of their strings on the ice to wet them, then let kids take turns trying this trick. Encourage children to perform the devotion for family and friends. Remind them to explain that our goal is to stick to Jesus, but we need to know how. Have them tell their audiences ways we can stick to Jesus.

Extra Excitement

● Play a zany game of Sticky-Ball. Wad up a two-foot length of masking tape to make a sticky-ball. Hand the ball to one player who will toss the sticky-ball at another player. Have the other kids hop on one foot to avoid being tagged by the sticky-ball. If someone is tagged, he or she becomes the next sticky-ball tosser.

● Let kids make unusual paintings using food coloring, ice cubes, and salt. Have kids place a few drops of food coloring on their papers, then use an ice cube to spread the colors. While the paintings are still wet, invite kids to sprinkle salt on their papers. As the salt and water dry, the pictures take on a nifty, sparkly appearance.

TRICKY TIPS

✳ Be sure you count to fifteen so the ice begins to melt and attach to the string.

✳ Keep the ice cubes in the freezer until you're ready to begin your devotion.

Permission to photocopy this activity granted for local church use. Copyright © Susan L. Lingo.
Published in *"Show Me!" Devotions for Leaders to Teach Kids* by Group Publishing, Inc.,
P.O. Box 481, Loveland, CO 80539.

GOAL GETTER:
This memorable feat of "fantabulism" helps kids understand that our lives become changed when we accept Jesus as our Savior.

VERSE TO VIEW:
2 Corinthians 3:18

TRICKS OF THE TRADE:
You'll need a Bible, a two-liter plastic bottle, water, half-inch plastic tubing, black spray paint, scissors, putty, black electrical tape, red and green food coloring, a pitcher, a clear drinking glass, and a small margarine tub.

The Grand Finale: Changed Forever!

The Dynamite Devotion

To accomplish this bit of awesome amazement, you'll need to prepare a simple bottle prop. This breathtaking bottle requires a little preparation and drying time, but once done will delight kids (and adults) for years. It's worth it!

First, remove the top half of a two-liter plastic bottle. Cut a half-inch hole in the side of the bottle about three inches from the top. Paint the outside of the bottle with black spray paint, and let the bottle dry completely. Cut a four-inch length of plastic tubing to fit in the hole, then run a bit of putty or florist's clay around the hole to seal any openings. Secure the tube to the bottle by wrapping black electrical tape around the entire tube and around the putty on the bottle. You're almost ready! Just before the devotion, fill the bottle to just below the hole with water. Add green food coloring to the water. Now fill a pitcher with water and add red food coloring (a clear pitcher is most effective). Float a small margarine tub in the bottle. Whew! *Now* you're ready to begin!

Place the bottle, the pitcher of red water, and a clear drinking glass on a table. Turn the bottle so that the "spout" (plastic tube) is sideways to the audience, then position the drinking glass under the spout. Say: **Some changes in life are good. For instance, it's good to change socks or a burned-out light bulb. What are some other good changes in life?** Allow time for kids to tell their ideas. Then say: **The Bible tells us about a change**

side view

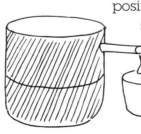

that's so special and powerful, it changes our lives forever. You'll never be the same again! Let's find out about that change.

Have a volunteer read aloud 2 Corinthians 3:18. Then slowly pour the red water into the plastic bowl floating in the bottle. Be careful to keep the red water in the bowl and make sure the children can't see the bowl! Say: **When we believe in Jesus and ask him to forgive us, he changes our lives forever!** As you pour, the weight of the margarine tub causes a rising water level in the bottle, and green water will pour from the spout into the drinking glass! **We're never the same again!** When the glass is full of green water, ask:

● **In what ways are we changed when we accept Jesus?**

● **How can we ask Jesus to forgive us and change our lives forever?** Invite kids to ask Jesus into their lives in a way that's appropriate to your church's traditions, then close with a prayer: **Dear Lord, thank you for being our friend and loving Savior. We're so glad our lives are changed because of your love. In Jesus' name, amen.**

Explain the trick and demonstrate how it works. Point out how putty was used to seal the opening. Then carefully pour the red water from the margarine tub back into the pitcher and the green water from the glass into the bottle. Let kids take turns pouring red water into the tub to create the "change." Encourage kids to make a bottle at home and perform the devotion for family and friends. Remind kids to explain that when we believe in Jesus as our Savior and friend, our lives are changed forever.

Extra Excitement

● Use this devotion to serve a memorable snack. Instead of green water, pour chilled apple juice into the bottle. Let kids each pour a bit of water into the margarine tub and let juice pour into a paper cup. Serve small cookies or crackers with the beverage.

TRICKY TIPS

✳ Older kids might enjoy the symbolism of the colored water. Explain that the red water represents the blood Jesus shed for our sins, and the green water is the new, growing life we have when we accept Jesus as our Savior.

✳ If your class is small, prepare a bottle for each child. Or let older kids make their own bottles over the course of two weeks.

Everyday Clay

GOAL GETTER:
Form funky clay in this fun devotional, and learn that God molds us as he desires.

VERSES TO VIEW:
Romans 9:21-22a

TRICKS OF THE TRADE:
You'll need a Bible, liquid starch, a tablespoon, white craft glue, clear packing tape, and small resealable plastic bags.

The Dynamite Devotion

Set out liquid starch, a tablespoon, and the white craft glue. Hand each child a small resealable plastic bag. Say: **When we're born into the world, we're like these empty bags. We don't have a lot of things in our lives yet, and we don't have lots of experience doing things or feeling certain ways. Our lives are waiting to be filled, and it's important to fill them with things God desires. God is our Maker, and he molds and shapes us to become special. We're like clay, and God is like the Potter molding us into special beings. Let's read what the Bible tells us about being God's clay.**

Read aloud Romans 9:21-22a. Then ask:

● **Why is it good that God molds us as he desires?**

● **How is God molding your life right now?**

Say: **God shapes each of us in special ways, just as a potter shapes different kinds of vases and pots from clay. Let's make some unusual clay, and see what you can mold and shape.**

Using the tablespoon, measure three spoonfuls of liquid starch and two spoonfuls of craft glue into each plastic bag. Be sure to seal the bags tightly, then fold over the top edge of each bag and seal it with clear packing tape.

Instruct children to gently knead the mixture in their bags until it forms a squishy mass. Then invite children to make things with the putty while it's in the bag. Circulate and ask children questions such as "Why do you think God wants to make you someone special who can serve him in lots of ways?" and "What's one way you can serve God this week?" Encourage children to tell about the shapes they're molding.

After a few minutes, say: **God makes us into many shapes, just as we're making lots of shapes with our putty. God is the Potter, and we're his clay. We want God to mold us and make us into people he can use in lots of special ways. Take your clay home, and encourage a friend or someone in your family to make a shape that shows how God is molding him or her.**

Remind children to keep their plastic bags sealed and to throw them away when the clay becomes stale and hard.

Extra Excitement

• Make and mold different kinds of clay. Try using ready-made clay or florists' clay, or make your own clay by mixing equal parts of baking soda and salt, adding enough water to form a malleable mixture. For interesting textures, add rice, sawdust, or sand. Keep clay in plastic bags or airtight margarine tubs.

• Edible clay is a *real* treat! Mix one-third of a jar of peanut butter with one box of powdered sugar. Knead until the dough is soft and pliable. Encourage kids to mold edible statues of what they think God is making them into, then have them gobble up their sweet creations.

TRICKY TIPS

✳ Be sure to use new plastic bags so there are no holes. This putty-clay is non-toxic—but not tasty, either!

✳ Use the modeling clay or putty activity to illustrate the story of Creation (Genesis 1–2), how wonderfully God has made us (Psalm 139), or how Jesus wants to mold us into fishers of men (Mark 1:17).

Topsy-Turvy

Step 1
Hold up the picture.

Step 2
Fold top of the paper down.

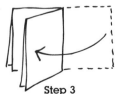

Step 3
Fold the right side forward to the left.

The Dynamite Devotion

Before this devotion, photocopy the "Strong-Stander" handout from page 82 for each child. This devotion is a story you tell while folding and unfolding the sheet of paper. Practice the story and folding directions so you can present the devotion without reading the story. You don't need to memorize the story, just retell it in your own words as you fold and unfold the paper. Be sure to hold the paper in front of you so it's facing your audience as you tell the story.

Say: **Have you ever had a bad day? I mean a *really* bad day?** (Step 1) **Well, let me tell you a story about a boy named Sam, who had a really bad day, and how he turned it around.**

Step 2: **Sam woke up late one morning. He jumped out of bed and rushed to get ready for school. He was in such a hurry that he brushed his teeth with deodorant instead of toothpaste! Sam didn't forget to brush his teeth, but he did forget to do something very important!**

Step 3: **Everything went wrong for Sam that day! He got in a fight with his best friend. He lost his lunch money. And he tripped over his shoelace and fell in a puddle.**

Step 4: **What was wrong? What had he forgotten that was so important? Why did Sam feel so turned around and . . .**

Step 5: **. . . UPSIDE DOWN?**

Step 6: **As Sam climbed into bed that night, he pulled the covers up . . .**

Step 7: **. . . snuggled down, and closed his eyes.**

Step 8: **In a flash, Sam knew what he'd forgotten!**

Step 9: **Sam had forgotten to start the day talking to God through prayer! Maybe tomorrow would be better if he started the day with prayer.**

Step 10: **So Sam prayed. He asked God to help him remember to pray, and asked God to keep him right-side up and right happy inside!**

Say: **It was pretty amazing to turn a paper upside down without flipping the paper over, wasn't it? But**

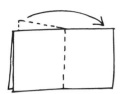

Step 4
Fold the side facing
you back to the
front.

Step 5
Open up.

Step 6
Fold top of the
paper down.

Step 7
Fold the right side to
the left side.

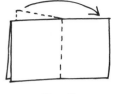

Step 8
Fold the side facing
the audience back to
your right.

praying brings even more amazing things! When we
pray, God always listens, and he answers, too. Listen to
what the Bible says about praying.

Read aloud Psalm 91:14-16. Then say: **Praying helps
us stand strong in the power of God. There's power in
prayer, and we need to remember to pray often!**

Distribute photocopies of the "Strong-Stander" handout. Demonstrate the trick as you teach the children how
to fold and unfold their papers. Allow the kids to get into
pairs and tell each other the devotional story as they try
the trick a few times. Encourage children to perform this
devotion for family and friends. Remind children to tell
people that there's superstrength in daily prayer.

Step 9
Open up.

Step 10
Hold up the picture.

Extra Excitement

● To reinforce the importance of
prayer, design a prayer poster. Let
kids trace their hands on poster
board, then color and decorate the hands using paints,
markers, Bingo daubers, and glitter glue. Title the poster,
"We're Praying for YOU!" Have children write people's
names on the poster each time they'd like that person
prayed for. See how many people your class can pray for
over the next month. Be sure to ask for praise reports on
how those people are doing!

● Let kids enjoy a rousing game of Prayer Tag. Draw
pairs of praying hands on paper plates, then tape the
plates around the floor. Choose a child to be "It," and
play the game like regular tag. Inform children of the following rules: they must hop or walk heel-to-toe, they
can't be tagged when they're standing on a paper
prayer plate, and only one person to a plate at any time.

TRICKY TIPS

✳ Use this same trick,
and fold a dollar bill to
illustrate how love of
money can turn you
upside down. Remind
your audience that God
loves a cheerful giver
and that God is always
our number one focus—
not material wealth.

Rainbow of Peace 'n' Love

OAL GETTER:
These colorful creations will help kids realize that God wants us to live in his peace.

ERSES TO VIEW:
Philippians 4:6-7

RICKS OF THE TRADE:
You'll need a Bible, newspapers, muffin pans, food coloring, water, a one-half teaspoon, and coffee filters or paper towels.

The Dynamite Devotion

Cover a table with newspapers. Set out muffin pans and coffee filters or paper towels. Be sure to provide at least two coffee filters for each child. Add one-half teaspoon of food coloring to each muffin cup, then fill each cup with water. Use a variety of colors! Fold the coffee filter you'll use in half two or three times before you begin.

Gather the kids around the table. Ask:

● **When have you had an argument or a fight with someone? How did it feel?**

● **What would it be like if everyone in the world disagreed and fought all the time?**

Say: **We read in the newspapers and hear on the news about people fighting all over the world. People often think they're the only ones who are right and want everyone to agree with them. Do you know someone like that? Have you ever felt the same way?** Hold the coffee filter by the point and slightly dip one edge of the coffee filter in the colored water. Do not use yellow.

Sometimes we forget that God made each of us different and that it's fine to disagree— but not to fight. God wants us to be different just as he created us—but he also wants us to be the same in two ways: loving him (slightly dip another corner or edge of the filter in a different color, but not yellow), **and living peacefully with each other.** Dip one last piece of the filter in another color, and slightly dip the point of the filter in yellow.

Carefully unfold the coffee filter as you say: **Do you know what happens when we love God and treat each other with kindness?** Hold up the coffee filter. There should be a yellow splotch in the center of swirling colors. Point to the yellow center and say: **God's peace surrounds us, and his love is in the center of our lives! Let's read about God's peace and how it affects us.**

Have a volunteer read aloud Philippians 4:6-7. Then ask:

● **How can God's love and peace make your life better?**

● **How can you have more of God's peace in your life?**

● **In what ways can you live more peacefully with others?**

Hand each child a coffee filter, and explain how you folded the filter. Then invite kids to lightly dip their own coffee filters in food coloring. Remind kids to "dip the tip" in yellow. Let everyone make two colorful coffee filters. Then encourage kids to each present one of their "peaceful papers" to another person as they explain about God's perfect peace.

Extra Excitement

● Create a colorful display for a church hall or entryway. Be sure to have kids write "God" in the yellow centers of their coffee filters. Title your gallery, "God Is the Center of It All."

● Line up at one end of the playing area, and assign each child a color of the rainbow (red, orange, yellow, green, blue, or purple). Choose one child to be the Tagger, and have him or her stand in the center of the playing area. Have the Tagger call out a color, then all the kids assigned that color hop to the opposite side of the classroom or playing area. The Tagger can hop around tagging players who then become Taggers to help catch others. Play until everyone has been caught.

TRICKY TIPS

✳ You may wish to use plastic sandwich bags on kids' hands to keep their fingers from being colored by the food coloring.

✳ Lay the dyed coffee filters on newspapers to dry. Iron the filters with a warm iron if they become wrinkled after drying and you plan to display them.

Bridge to Heaven

GOAL GETTER:

This fascinating devotion will teach kids about the bridge Jesus makes between God and people.

VERSE TO VIEW:

John 14:6

TRICKS OF THE TRADE:

You'll need a Bible, an envelope of unflavored gelatin, a balloon, a wool sock or mitten, and a paper plate.

The Dynamite Devotion

Pour an envelope of unflavored gelatin in the center of a paper plate. Blow up and tie off a balloon. Place the paper plate of gelatin, the balloon, the wool sock, and the Bible on a table. Have kids stand around the table, and ask:

● **How are bridges useful?**

● **What would it be like if there were no bridges in the world?**

Say: **Today I want to tell you about a very special bridge between God and people. Let's pretend the gelatin on this plate represents all people. There are lots of them! Let's also pretend that this balloon represents God.** Hold the balloon about a foot above the plate, and say: **When God created people, he loved them so much, but people disobeyed God and became separated from him. See the space between God and us?**

Rub the balloon on the wool sock as you continue: **God knew we needed a way to draw close to him. So God sent Jesus to be a special bridge!** Hold the balloon a few inches over the gelatin. Bits of gelatin should rise to create "bridges" between the paper plate and the balloon. **When we have faith in Jesus, he becomes the bridge that connects us to God. And we can have a relationship with God!**

Set down the balloon, and have a volunteer read aloud John 14:6. Ask:

● **Why do people need Jesus as a bridge to God?**

● **How does Jesus bridge the gap between God and us?**

● **How can you let Jesus be your own bridge to God?**

Explain how this trick works, then allow each person a turn holding the balloon over the gelatin to make "bridges." Encourage kids to present this simple devotion to family and friends. Remind them to explain that Jesus is our special bridge to God.

Extra Excitement

● Invite kids to use flavored gelatin to make delicious "Jesus Jewels" gumdrops. Give each child a paper plate and a plastic fork. Pour several one-inch piles of fruit-flavored gelatin powder on each paper plate. Use flavors such as blueberry, lime, cherry, and lemon. Then add three or four drops of water to each gelatin pile. Instruct kids to stir each pile until the gelatin forms rubbery little "gumdrops." Remind kids that Jesus is the one who bridges the gap between people and God.

● Set out paper and tape, and challenge kids to build bridges between items such as chairs, tables, or even walls! Have kids build in pairs or small groups. When they're finished, let kids tell about their bridges, then explain why Jesus is the most special "bridge" of all.

TRICKY TIPS

✳ Be sure to use unflavored gelatin for the devotion. Fruit-flavored gelatin will not make bridges—it will just fly to the balloon and stick.

Hidden in Your Heart

GOAL GETTER:
This devotion is as fun to make as it is to eat, and it teaches kids the importance of taking God's Word into their hearts.

VERSE TO VIEW:
Psalm 119:11

TRICKS OF THE TRADE:
You'll need a Bible, candy hearts, prepared cake batter, a cookie sheet, spoons, an ice-cream cone for each child (use cones that have flat bottoms), and access to an oven.

The Dynamite Devotion

One person can present this devotion, but pairs of kids can prepare the cupcakes. Place ice-cream cones, cake batter, spoons, candy hearts, and a cookie sheet on a table. Gather kids and ask:

● **Why do people sometimes keep feelings and thoughts in their hearts?**

● **What kinds of things do you keep in your heart?**

Say: **Did you know that God wants us to keep something special in our hearts? Let's read what the Bible tells us about that special thing. When you think you know what God wants in our hearts, cover your heart with your hands.**

Read aloud Psalm 119:11. Then ask:

● **What special thing does God want us to take in, then keep in our hearts?**

● **Why does God want us to take his Word into us?**

● **How can we keep God's Word in our hearts?**

Say: **God's Word is always true and never-changing. God tells us how to live and love and treat other people.**

God's Word is so important that he wants us to understand it and keep it in our hearts so that it can change our lives. When we take God's Word to heart, it helps us live as God desires. Let's make Down-in-Our-Hearts cupcakes with special hidden surprises inside.

Let kids spoon cake batter into ice-cream cones, then use the end of a spoon to push a candy heart deep in the batter. As kids work, make comments such as "Having God's Word in our hearts helps us live like God wants us to live" and "When we learn God's Word, we can apply it to our lives." Place the cones in an upright position on a cookie sheet, then carefully slide the cookie sheet into a 325 degree oven. Bake the cupcakes for about fifteen minutes or until the cake springs back.

As the cupcakes bake and cool, do one or both of the Extra Excitement activities below.

When the cupcakes cool, say: **Now let's nibble our special treats to find the hidden surprises. As you eat, remember that God's Word is the most special treat we can keep in our hearts!**

Extra Excitement

● Older kids will enjoy making Scripture hearts to exchange. Give each child a sheet of construction paper, and have him or her cut out a large heart shape. Then let each child choose a verse from the Bible and copy it onto his or her paper heart. Instruct the children to cut the hearts into ten puzzle pieces. Form pairs, and have kids exchange the paper-heart puzzles and put them together. Then let each child read aloud the verse on his or her puzzle.

● Let younger children play a game of Who Has the Heart? Choose a child to sit in a chair facing away from the rest of the children, and place a candy heart behind him or her. Then silently tap a child to sneak forward and snatch the candy heart. Have all the children cover their hearts with their hands. Let the child sitting in the chair turn around and have two guesses to find the hidden heart. Have the child with the hidden heart be the next player to sit in the "guessing seat."

TRICKY TIPS

✳ For colorful fun, let kids decorate their cupcakes with canned icing and candy sprinkles.

Fueled Up

GOAL GETTER:

Kids will love making these awesome "rockets" as they learn that God's power fuels us to serve him.

VERSE TO VIEW:

Zechariah 4:6

TRICKS OF THE TRADE:

You'll need a Bible, plastic soda pop bottles, corks to fit the bottles, crepe paper, tape, paper cups and towels, a box of baking soda, a teaspoon, a half-cup measuring cup, water, and vinegar.

The Dynamite Devotion

This devotion is intended for older kids in an outdoor setting.

Before class, make a "Fueled Flyer" by taping six-inch-long crepe paper streamers to a cork. Be sure the cork fits snugly into the top of your plastic bottle. Place a half cup of water and a half cup of vinegar into separate paper cups. Now place a teaspoon of baking soda in the center of a four-inch-square piece of paper towel. Roll up the paper towel, and twist the ends to keep the baking soda inside. Set the paper towel with baking soda aside. You're now ready to "fly"!

Gather kids outside in an open area. Set down the bottle, cork, paper towel containing baking soda, and the paper cups of water and vinegar. Ask:

● **What fuels a rocket?**

● **How far would a rocket fly if it didn't have fuel or had the wrong kind of fuel?**

Say: **Did you know we're kind of like rockets when it comes to serving God? We need fuel to serve God, but it's a different kind of fuel than rockets need. Let's see what the Bible tells us.** Have a volunteer read aloud Zechariah 4:6. Then ask:

● **What fuels us to serve God?**

● **How does God's Spirit give us power to serve?**

● **What's one way you can serve God this week?**

Say: **God tells us to rely on his Spirit to fuel us. When we have God's Spirit in us** (pour the water into the bottle), **a desire to do what God wants** (pour the vinegar into

the bottle), **and we rely on God's power** (place the paper towel containing the baking soda into the bottle and cork it tightly), **we're fueled to serve. We can say, "Stand back and watch us go for God!"** Have everyone stand clear of the bottle and wait for the cork to fly upward. (It may take several seconds for the liquid to soak through to the baking soda.)

After the cork rockets skyward, invite kids to make their own Fueled Flyers. Be sure to remind kids to stand clear after adding the paper towel with baking soda. Encourage kids to demonstrate their fabulous flyers to family and friends, and remind them to tell those people about how God's Spirit fuels us to serve him.

Extra Excitement

● Have a contest to see how far the fancy corks fly, how high they go, and how fast they take off. Have kids name ways to serve God each time their rockets take off. Give everyone a blue crepe paper ribbon for being "fueled-up" to serve God!

● Younger kids would enjoy watching this devotion, then making their own form of Fueled Flyer. Have kids tape crepe paper streamers to the bottoms of balloons. Help them tie strings to the balloons, then run outside to let them fly.

TRICKY TIPS

✳ Though the Fueled Flyers have relatively little "power," remind kids to stand back after the baking soda has been added.

✳ Be sure corks fit snugly in the tops of the bottles to ensure good "launches."

Butter Me Up

The Dynamite Devotion

Place the whipping cream, crackers, plastic knives, Bible, and the jar and lid on a table. Gather kids near the table. Ask:

- **What is "trust?"**
- **When do you need to trust someone?**
- **What happens when you're not willing to trust?**

Say: **It's not always easy to trust and have patience. We often want things to happen quickly and smoothly, without any wait. Sometimes we're not even patient with God. We pray and expect God to act right away. And sometimes, when we don't think God acts quickly enough, we become angry. God wants us to be patient and trust him. Now I want you to help me make something delicious to eat, but we'll have to have patience to make it. You'll have to trust me that we'll eventually have fresh butter.**

Open the pint of cream and pour it into the jar. Screw the lid on tightly, and shake the jar rapidly and firmly. Say: **We'll take turns shaking this jar and see what happens. Meanwhile, let's read what the Bible tells us about trusting.** Pass the jar to someone else to shake, then continue passing and shaking the jar for the next five minutes or until the butter separates from the buttermilk.

Ask a volunteer to read aloud Isaiah 40:31. Continue shaking the jar and ask:

- **Who are we to be patient with and trust in?**
- **What happens when we trust in God?**
- **Why is trusting God important?**
- **How can you trust God more this week?**

Say: **God promises that if we're patient and trust him, we'll have the strength we need. Are you about ready to rest from shaking this jar? Let's see what our trust and waiting has done.** Open the jar. If the butter is not in a lump at the bottom of it,

replace the lid and continue shaking the jar. When the lump of butter forms, place it on the jar lid. Hand each child several crackers and a plastic knife.

As kids spread butter on their crackers, say: **Trust in God is so important! God does things in his own time, and it's up to us to trust him and be patient. When we do, things turn out great—like our butter!**

Tell kids again how to make butter. Remember to tell them it's important to have patience shaking the jar—it takes time for the butter to form. Then encourage kids to present this devotion to their families and friends. Remind kids to tell others that we're to trust and wait upon God in all we do.

Extra Excitement

● Let kids each make decorative pats of butter to share with their families. Make a batch of butter, then add a few drops of yellow food coloring to the butter. Mix it well, then use a plastic spoon to spread the butter in plastic candy molds. Chill the "pats" of butter for a few minutes in the freezer. Pop out the butter, then wrap four to six pats in aluminum foil. Let each child make a small package of butter pats to take home.

TRICKY TIPS

✳ Shaking the jar may take quite a while—up to ten minutes. But that's what patience and trust are all about!

The Amazing No-Leak Bottle

The Dynamite Devotion

Before this devotion, decorate the neck of a plastic soda pop bottle with colored vinyl tape. You can find colored vinyl tape at hardware stores.

Set the plastic bottle, bottle cap, a pushpin, a Bible, a dishpan, and a pitcher of water on a table. Gather kids around the table. Ask:

● **What keeps you safe?**

● **How could you be safer?**

Say: **There are lots of things we do to keep ourselves safe.** Pour water into the bottle, and fill it up as you continue talking. **Some people claim that alarms, weapons, and common sense will keep us safe. But do they really? What happens when really big troubles come along?** Allow kids to tell their ideas.

Then say: **Big troubles can come along and really hurt us.** Use the pushpin to carefully poke a hole near the bottom of the bottle. The water will spout from the hole, so hold the bottle over a dishpan!

Say: **Wow! Look what happens to us! We can't do anything to stop the flow of hurt. But if we remember that God protects us** (pour in a bit more water), **and we trust in him,** (screw on the bottle top), **he'll stop the hurt!** Set the bottle down in the dishpan. Then say: **Now let's see what the Bible tells us about God's protection.**

Have a volunteer read aloud Psalm 41:1-3. Then ask:

● **Why does God protect us?**

● **Does this passage say we'll never be sick or get hurt? Explain.**

● **In what ways does God protect us?**

● **How can you trust in God's protection this week?**

Pick up the bottle without squeezing it, and say: **With**

God's protection and our trust in him, we can face any problem. **But when we just trust in ourselves** (remove the bottle top), **the hurt will flow. Remember, when we trust in God** (replace the bottle top), **he protects us!**

Explain how you prepared the plastic bottle and how the water will stop only when the bottle top is securely placed on the bottle. Hand each child a plastic bottle, and have kids form pairs or small groups. Invite kids to decorate their bottles with the colored vinyl tape, then hand each child a plastic pushpin. Have an adult push each pin in the bottle. Tell kids to leave the push-pins in place until they're ready to show what happens to "false strength." Encourage kids to present this devotion to their families and friends. Remind them to tell their audiences that God will protect us in whatever problems we face.

Extra Excitement

● Challenge kids to a game of "protection" bowling. Set empty plastic bottles in the center of the room, and form two bowling teams. Give each team a foam ball, and let teams take turns bowling over the plastic "pins" while the other team tries to protect the pins.

TRICKY TIPS

✳ Clear pushpins work best for this devotion because they're unnoticeable when poked in the bottle.

✳ Be sure to fill the bottle full of water for the best visual effect!

Crazy Cookie Bags

The Dynamite Devotion

Place the Bible, peanut butter, powdered sugar, oatmeal, raisins, tablespoons, and resealable sandwich bags on a table. Ask:

● **How are the ingredients on the table like people? How are they different?**

● **Why do you think God created people differently?**

● **Who is God's family?**

● **How are God's family members alike? different?**

Say: **God made everyone different and special. Each one of us has unique talents, gifts, and abilities.** Point to the ingredients you've gathered. **We can think of these ingredients as the different gifts God gives each of us. What do you think happens when we mix them all together? Let's see!**

Hand each person a resealable plastic sandwich bag. Show kids how to add each of the following ingredients to their bags: one spoonful of peanut butter, four spoonfuls of powdered sugar, two spoonfuls of oatmeal, and one spoonful of raisins. Show kids how to seal their bags securely. Tell kids not to mix the ingredients in their bags.

When everyone has prepared a bag, say: **All these different ingredients are ready to be mixed. But first, what do you think happens when God's people mix their talents, gifts, and abilities together?** Pause for kids to tell their ideas. Then have a volunteer read aloud Ephesians 4:11-13. Ask:

● **How does mixing talents and gifts help God's family serve God better?**

● **Is one gift or talent better than another? Explain.**

● **What gifts or talents can you use in God's family?**

Say: **If we put only one ingredient in our bags, it**

wouldn't taste nearly as good as all the ingredients mixed together. It's that way with God's family, too. When all of us mix our talents, gifts, and abilities, we can serve God in many ways. Now let's mix the ingredients in our bags to make delicious cookies-in-a-bag to eat.

After kids have eaten their cookies, hand each child a fresh sandwich bag and a copy of the recipe to take home. Encourage kids to share this delicious devotion with their families and friends. Remind kids to tell others that we all have different talents and gifts to add to God's family.

Extra Excitement

● Let kids create unique torn-paper "cookies." Show kids how to tear a large cookie shape from brown construction paper. Let kids glue on torn-paper raisins, peanuts, candy sprinkles, cherries, and other "delectables." Then mix white powdered tempera paint with white craft glue. Let kids drizzle a bit of fake frosting over their paper cookies. After the cookies are dry, let kids write various talents, gifts, and abilities they have on the paper cookies.

TRICKY TIPS

✱ Be sure to check each plastic bag before mixing the ingredients to make sure the bag is sealed tightly.

✱ If mixtures seem a little sticky, add more powdered sugar. If they're too crumbly, add a bit more peanut butter.

The Miraculous Multiplying Circle

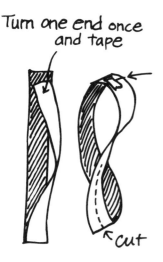

Turn one end once and tape

← cut

The Dynamite Devotion

Before this devotion, cut enough eleven-by-two-inch construction paper strips for each child to have five. Use a variety of colors for extra fun. A paper cutter will speed up the process.

Place the paper strips, tape, Bible, and scissors on a table. Gather kids and ask:

● **What happens when you call a friend on the telephone and tell him or her something really exciting? Does that person call others?**

● **How far do you think a great message travels?**

Hold up a paper strip. Say: **This paper strip has two ends just like a telephone. When someone tells another person something really exciting, such as how much God loves them, they have a connection!** Give the paper strip a twist, then tape the ends together. Carefully poke the scissors in the center of the paper strip, then begin cutting lengthwise down the center. Keep the loop held together as you cut. Continue snipping and say: **God's love forms a circle around these people. But it doesn't stop there! When those people tell others, watch what happens.**

When you've cut all the way around the loop one time, set down the scissors. Hold the loop together and say: **Before we see what exciting thing happens when we tell others about God, let's read what the Bible tells us about spreading God's message.** Have someone read aloud Matthew 28:19-20. Then ask:

● **Who needs to hear about God's love?**

● **Why is it important to tell others about Jesus?**

● **What did Jesus promise he would do as we tell others about him?**

● **Who can you tell about Jesus this week?**

Say: **Now let's see what happens when we tell others about Jesus.** Let the loop stretch downward. It should have doubled in size! Say: **Wow! The circle grew! When we tell others about Jesus, we please God and spread his love to other people.**

Give three paper strips to each child. Let kids form pairs or trios and try this trick on their own. Invite kids to make three "circle of love" loops to get the hang of taping and cutting the paper strips. Then hand each child two more paper strips to take home. Encourage kids to present this devotion to families and friends. Remind them to tell their audiences that we please God and spread his love when we tell others about him.

Extra Excitement

● Older kids will love the challenge of cutting various sizes of paper loops to see how large the "circle of love" will grow. Have kids tape together two or three lengths of paper to make a loop. Let kids cut in pairs and compare the sizes of the circles made. Point out how God's circle of love has no end—it just goes 'round and 'round forever!

● Younger children will enjoy making "circle of love" mobiles. Invite children to cut through five or six colorful loops, then tape them to a clothes hanger. Tie curling ribbon to the corners of the hanger for a festive touch. Consider using different papers, such as gift-wrap or wallpaper for the loops.

TRICKY TIPS

✳ Make sure you give the paper strip a twist before taping the ends together.

Color-Changing Paint

GOAL GETTER:

This crafty devotion will teach kids that Jesus' light cuts through the darkness of our lives.

VERSE TO VIEW:

John 8:12

TRICKS OF THE TRADE:

You'll need a Bible, black construction paper, cotton swabs, newspaper, paper bowls, and bleach. You might also want old shirts to protect children's clothing from the bleach.

The Dynamite Devotion

Cover a table with newspaper. Set out bowls of bleach, cotton swabs, and the black construction paper. Darken the room as much as possible. Gather kids near the table and ask:

● **When have you been afraid of the dark?**
● **What's scary about darkness?**

Hold up a sheet of black construction paper. Ask:

● **How is this sheet of construction paper like the darkness?**

Say: **It's often scary when we're surrounded by darkness. Shadows seem to follow us and it's hard to find our way when we can't see clearly. It's like that in our lives, too.** Ask:

● **How are being confused and scared like being in the dark?**

● **What happens to our lives when we're in the dark?**

● **Is there any light strong enough to take away all the darkness in the world? Explain.**

Say: **Living in confusion, fear, worry, and doubt can steal away our happiness and stop us from finding our way to Jesus. We need help!** Turn up the lights a bit. Invite kids to stand by the table. Dip a cotton swab in bleach, then say: **Watch what happens when I add Jesus' light to the darkness.** Make a cross on the black paper. A bright orange color will appear wherever the bleach touches. Say: **Wow! Jesus' light cuts through the darkness, and everything is brighter and clearer.** Dip the cotton swab in the bleach, and "paint" a sun on the paper. Say: **God's Son brings light to the world and chases away the darkness in our lives.** Once more dip the cotton swab in bleach, then paint a happy face on the paper. Say: **Jesus**

turns our sadness to gladness. Let's read what the Bible says about Jesus as the light of the world.

Ask a volunteer to read aloud John 8:12. Then ask:

● **In what ways is Jesus a light to the world?**

● **What happens when Jesus' light comes into your life?**

● **How can Jesus chase away the darkness in your life?**

Say: **Jesus is the light of the world. His love and power shine through the darkness and show us the way to God. Let's paint pictures to remind us that Jesus' light shines through the darkness.**

Invite kids to each paint a picture using bleach and cotton swabs. Caution kids not to get any bleach on clothes or skin. (If bleach gets on hands, rinse with water.) As kids paint their pictures, encourage them to present this striking devotion to their families and friends. Remind them to tell others that Jesus' love and power light up the world.

Extra Excitement

● Young children will especially enjoy singing favorite songs such as "Shine, Jesus, Shine" and "This Little Light of Mine." Have children pass flashlights to each other as they sing.

● Celebrate Jesus' light with festive cupcakes. Bake the cupcakes in advance, then let children frost and decorate them. Add "you can't blow 'em out" candles on top. Light the candles for the children, and have them try blowing them out. As the candles relight, have everyone say, "Jesus' light shines on me!"

TRICKY TIPS

✳ Hang the finished pictures in a hallway and title the display: "Jesus' Light Shines Through the Darkness."

Confusion Cookies

GOAL GETTER:

This delightful devotion helps kids realize that even if God's ways seem confusing to us, he knows what he's doing.

VERSES TO VIEW:

Isaiah 55:8-9;
1 Corinthians 1:25

TRICKS OF THE TRADE:

You'll need a Bible, a nine-by-twelve-inch pan, and the following ingredients: ½ cup melted butter, 1 cup of crushed graham crackers, 1 cup of flaked coconut, 1 cup chopped nuts, 1 12-ounce package of chocolate chips, and 1 can of sweetened condensed milk. You'll also need access to an oven.

The Dynamite Devotion

Place the pan on one end of a table, then set out the ingredients in the same order in which they're listed in the margin.

Gather kids and say: **We're going to make a batch of crazy Confusion Cookies. Usually we follow directions and mix and add and stir different ingredients together. But today we're just going to pour ingredients on top of each other and bake them!**

Have kids get into small groups. Then have groups take turns layering the ingredients in the pan. First the butter, then the crushed graham crackers, the coconut, the nuts, the chocolate chips, and finally, the condensed milk. As kids layer the ingredients, make comments such as "This is a confusing way to bake, isn't it?" and "How can these cookies be any good if we don't follow a recipe?"

When all the ingredients have been added, bake in a 325 degree oven for about 25 minutes, or until cookies are golden brown. As the cookies bake, ask:

● **When have you been confused about something?**

● **How did it feel to be mixed up?**

● **Who helped you figure things out or solve your problem?**

Say: **Sometimes we get confused. We might not understand why teachers tell us to write a certain way, or why parents say we can't go to a movie. We want to know "why?" We sometimes feel that way about God, too. It's hard to understand why God sometimes doesn't help someone get well or why he lets a robber get away. It's pretty confusing and makes us feel like asking, "Why, God?"** Ask:

● **Have you ever asked, "Why, God?" Explain.**

● **Why do you think we don't always understand how God works?**

Say: **Let's see what the Bible tells us about God's wisdom and why he doesn't always do things we understand.** Have a volunteer read aloud Isaiah 55:8-9 and 1 Corinthians 1:25. Then say: **God's ways are different from ours—that's because he's wiser than anyone! We don't always understand how God works, but we can trust God.** Ask:

● **How are Confusion Cookies like trusting God?**

Say: **When we made our Confusion Cookies, you might not have understood why we just tossed ingredients together instead of mixing and measuring them. But we can trust things will turn out fine, just as we trust God to do what's best for us. Do you think our cookies will be OK? Let's taste our Confusion Cookies to see!**

Remove the cookies from the oven, and let them cool for a few minutes. Then cut the cookies into bars and enjoy! Give children each a copy of the ingredients, and encourage them to make Confusion Cookies for their families and friends. Remind children to tell others that we need to trust God's wisdom and know things will turn out the way he wants them to.

Extra Excitement

● Talk about "wise" sayings such as "An apple a day keeps the doctor away" and "A penny saved is a penny earned." Let kids get into small groups and discuss what they think the sayings mean. Then invite volunteers to read from Proverbs 12:19-20; 13:9; and 15:19. Point out that many of our wise sayings actually come from the Bible. Remind kids that God's wisdom is perfect and lasts forever.

● For a simple craft idea, let kids embellish the letters in the phrase "TRUST GOD." Draw big block letters on a sheet of paper, then make a photocopy for each child in class. Set out markers, crayons, sequins, glue, ribbon, lace, and bits of aluminum foil. Then invite kids to decorate their mini-posters any way they choose. Encourage kids to hang their posters in their rooms to remind them that we can trust God with our lives.

TRICKY TIPS

✱ Check the Confusion Cookies often as they bake to make sure they don't burn.

✱ You may wish to substitute one cup of raisins for the crushed nuts.

Listen Up!

GOAL GETTER:

This fun devotion will teach kids that sometimes we must be still to hear God speak to us.

VERSE TO VIEW:

Psalm 46:10

TRICKS OF THE TRADE:

You'll need a Bible, lemon juice, a plastic bowl, a lamp, cotton swabs, and paper.

The Dynamite Devotion

Before this devotion, dip a cotton swab in lemon juice and write the words, "God loves you" on a sheet of paper. Write the words in small letters. When the lemon juice dries, it will be invisible on the paper. This is your "secret message."

Pour lemon juice in a bowl and place it on a table along with paper, the Bible, and the secret message. Remove the lamp's shade and plug in the lamp, but don't turn it on yet. Gather kids and ask:

● **What are ways we communicate with others?**

● **Talking is one way to receive messages from another person. What are other ways we receive messages?**

Say: **Communicating with others is something we do every day. We talk to people, wave hello, and even whisper. Sometimes we sing or draw pictures or wink to send messages. I have a special message for you on this paper. What does it say?** Hold up the secret message. **What? You can't see the message? Maybe this will help.**

Turn on the lamp, and choose a volunteer to hold the paper over the lighted bulb. Have the volunteer move the paper back and forth across the bulb as you say: **God wants to get messages through to us, but sometimes we're too busy to notice. It's important to find ways to listen to God and look for his messages. Let's see what the Bible tells us about listening to God.**

Have a volunteer read aloud Psalm 46:10. Then ask:

● **How does God get messages to us?**

● **Why is it important to get God's messages?**

● **What might happen if we miss a message from God?**

● **How can we listen to God more carefully?**

Check the secret message. The heat from the bulb should turn the dried lemon juice a light brown color and make the message visible. When the message "appears," have the volunteer read it aloud. Then say: **God's messages are very important and not always easy for us to read or hear. We must find time to be still and listen to God. Then his messages will be clear to us.**

Hand each child a piece of paper and a cotton swab. Explain how to write with the "invisible ink," then encourage kids to write their own invisible messages. When the lemon juice dries, let them take turns running the paper above the light bulb to expose the messages. Encourage kids to present this devotion to their families and friends. Remind them to tell their audiences that we must look and listen carefully for God's messages.

Extra Excitement

● Let kids "paint" secret pictures with lemon juice. Set out white paper and muffin cups of lemon juice, and let kids use cotton swabs as paintbrushes. Encourage kids to paint pictures of times they may listen to God, such as when they're praying or at bedtime. Then invite kids to exchange papers or present the secret pictures to friends. Be sure to remind kids to tell their friends how to reveal the pictures—so they too can pass along the important news about listening to God.

TRICKY TIPS

✱ Don't hold the paper directly on the light bulb or the paper may scorch.

✱ Grapefruit juice will work for this devotion as well as lemon juice.

OAL GETTER:

This astounding devotion helps kids understand that Jesus bore the weight of the world on his shoulders—for us.

ERSES TO VIEW:

1 Peter 2:21-24

RICKS OF THE TRADE:

You'll need a hardcover Bible, markers, white paper, and tape.

Weight of the World

The Dynamite Devotion

Set the paper, tape, and Bible on a table. Gather kids and say: **I have a very weighty question for you.** Hold up the paper and the Bible. **Can the Bible balance on this single sheet of paper?** Allow kids to respond. Then set the Bible on the edge of the paper and catch it as it falls. Say: **Not so easy, is it? The weight of the book is so heavy that it squashes this sheet of paper. Look how many single pages are in this book. They may be single sheets of paper, but together they make the Bible very heavy.**

Stand the Bible on the table, and say: **Stand up. Now take a giant step backward if you've ever done anything wrong.** Pause. **Take another giant step backward if you've ever said anything mean.** Pause. **Look. All of us are standing far away from God's Word. That's because we've all sinned and done and said things that are wrong. If you counted all the wrong things we've all ever said or done, that would be a LOT! Just like a lot of pages in a book!** Have kids return to the table.

Hold up a new sheet of paper and the Bible. Say: **God sent Jesus to take those sins. But think how heavy all our sins are! How did Jesus bear all the weight of our sins?**

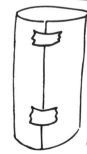

Tape the sheet of paper in a cylinder shape. Hold up the cylinder, and trace the circle shape at the end with your finger. Say: **Jesus' love for us has no end—just like a circle has no end! Jesus' love goes 'round and 'round and never ends.** Place the cylinder upright on the table, then gently lay the Bible so it balances on top. **Jesus' love for us was so strong, it held him up under the weight of all our sins. And Jesus lifted the heaviness of our sins up to God for forgiveness. Because Jesus**

carried our sins when he died on the cross, we can feel the lightness of freedom from sin!

Read aloud 1 Peter 2:21-24. Then ask:

● **How does it feel knowing Jesus took away our sins?**

● **How can you thank Jesus for taking away the wrong things you've said and done?**

Distribute paper, markers or crayons, and tape. Invite kids to work in pairs to make cylinders then use them to hold up their Bibles. Encourage kids to present this devotion to their families and friends. Remind them to tell others that Jesus bore the weight of our sins on the cross because he loves us so much.

Extra Excitement

● Let older kids experiment with folding and taping together various three-dimensional shapes such as stars, triangles, and rectangles. Supply an assortment of books to try balancing on the folded paper structures. Remind kids that no weight is greater than the sins Jesus bore for us—and no love stronger than his!

● Have children experience heaviness by holding their arms out from their sides for three minutes. As their outstretched arms are held up, read aloud 1 Peter 2:21-24. Then remind children that Jesus held all the bad things of the world because he loved us so much. Let children put their arms down at their sides, then close in a prayer thanking Jesus for taking away the heaviness of our sins.

TRICKY TIPS

✳ Use three or four pieces of tape to secure the cylinder. Be sure to tape across the seam, not parallel to it.

The Astounding X-Ray Tube

GOAL GETTER:
In this devotion, kids learn that God wants us to see through deception and lies to do what is right.

VERSES TO VIEW:
Philippians 1:9-10

TRICKS OF THE TRADE:
You'll need a Bible, cardboard tubes, and markers and crayons.

The Dynamite Devotion

Before this devotion, prepare an Astounding X-Ray Tube by decorating a cardboard tissue tube with markers and crayons. Empty bathroom tissue tubes are perfect, but you can make tubes from six-inch squares of poster board. You'll also need an undecorated tube for each child.

Set out the markers and crayons. Hand children each an "X-ray" tube, and invite them to decorate the tubes. As kids are working, ask:

● **When has someone lied to you or played a mean trick on you?**

● **How do you know when someone is telling a lie or being dishonest? How do you react?**

Say: **You're working on amazing X-ray tubes that will help you "see through" things. When you're finished, I'll explain. Then we'll learn about what God thinks of dishonesty and how he helps us see through lies.**

When children are finished making their X-ray tubes, have them set the tubes on the floor beside them.

Say: **Now let's try out our amazing X-ray tubes. With these astounding tubes, you can see right through your hand! Hold your tube in your left hand and put it up to your left eye. Now place your right hand beside the tube and look straight ahead as if you're looking at something far in the distance. Do you see a hole through your right palm?** Pause for kids to respond. Give a few extra moments if anyone is

having trouble "seeing" through their right hands.

Say: **Wow! You can see right through your hand. You know, when we know that someone isn't telling the truth or is trying to deceive us, we say that we can "see through" their lies. Sometimes our friends are dishonest or try to get us to do things that are wrong. God wants us to see through these lies and do the right thing. Let's read what the Bible says about being wise and seeing through lies.**

Ask a volunteer to read aloud Philippians 1:9-10. Then ask:

● **Why do you think God wants us to be wise and not taken in by lies?**

● **How does God help us see through lies and dishonesty?**

● **How can you be more wise about the things you do? the things you say?**

Say: **Our amazing X-ray tubes are pretty neat, but they're only a toy. God is the amazing one who helps us stay wise and see through lies!**

Let kids play with their X-ray tubes for a few minutes. Encourage them to present this devotion for their families and friends. Remind kids to tell others that God gives us wisdom to see through dishonesty and do the right thing.

Extra Excitement

● Play a fun game of I Spy a Lie. Have kids sit in a circle and hold their X-ray tubes. Choose one child to tell something true or make up something false. Tell kids it's OK to make up false statements for this game because they're going to practice "seeing through" lies. Truthful statements might include "I have blond hair" or "Baby kangaroos are called joeys." False statements might include "Fish breathe air" or "All people like dill pickles." When the kids spy a lie, have them shout "False!" through their X-ray tubes. If they spy a truthful statement, have them shout "True!" through their tubes.

TRICKY TIPS

✱ If kids have trouble "seeing through" their hands, remind them to look straight ahead as if they're looking far into the distance.

GOAL GETTER:
In this extraordinary devotion, kids learn what it means to be like Jesus.

VERSES TO VIEW:
2 Corinthians 3:16-18

TRICKS OF THE TRADE:
You'll need a Bible, scissors, three nine-by-twelve-inch pans, water, hydrogen peroxide, a black plastic trash bag, and photographic blueprint paper. You'll find photographic blueprint paper suppliers in the phone book under "Blueprints," or you can get it from most architects or builders.

The Grand Finale: Become Like Jesus

The Dynamite Devotion

In a darkened room, cut photographic blueprint paper into eight-inch squares. Be careful not to expose the paper to direct sunlight. After each square is cut, slide it into a black plastic trash bag to keep it in the dark.

This devotion is best suited to a sunny day where you can be outside. Place two pans of water on the grass. Pour hydrogen peroxide into the third pan and place it in between the pans of water. Keep the blueprint paper in the black bag and out of direct sunlight.

Gather kids and ask:

● **Why do we take photographs?**

● **How is a photograph like the person or thing being photographed? Explain.**

Say: **Did you know that God wants us to be like Jesus? What do you think that means?** Allow kids to tell their ideas. Then say: **Let's read what the Bible tells us about becoming like Jesus.**

Have a volunteer read aloud 2 Corinthians 3:16-18. Then ask:

● **Why would we want to be more like Jesus?**

● **How can we become more like Jesus?**

Say: **We want to be like Jesus in many ways—in the way we treat other people, the way we learn about God, the way we care for**

Water

Hydrogen Peroxide

Water

the sick, the way we give to those who need help, and the way we obey what God wants us to do. It's like we want to take a photograph of Jesus' heart and become like him. Let's take special photographs to remind us how important it is to become more like Jesus.

Have each person find several leaves, flowers, grasses, or twigs. Then one by one, hand each child a square of photographic blueprint paper. Have the children lay their papers in the sunlight and place their nature items on the paper. Instruct kids to hold the paper by the tips of the corners so the papers don't blow away. After three minutes, dip the papers in water, then peroxide, then water. Hang the papers to dry. You'll have beautiful prints of the nature items to frame!

If there's extra blueprint paper, hand each child a sheet in a black bag along with a copy of these instructions. Encourage kids to have their parents help with this devotion. Remind kids to tell their families that we want to become more like Jesus.

Extra Excitement

● Let kids decorate festive frames for their pictures. Hand each child an eight-inch square of poster board with a five-inch square cut from the center. Set out scissors and glue, and provide a variety of craft items such as ribbon, lace, rickrack, sequins, markers, and glitter glue. Use tape to attach the pictures so they show through the openings on the frames. Encourage kids to display their pictures at home as reminders of how we're to become more like Jesus.

● Take a cheery class picture and have it enlarged into a mini-poster. Most photocopy shops will enlarge photographs for a minimal price. If you'd rather, take individual pictures and glue them to a sheet of poster board for a poster. Then let the kids sign the poster and title it: "We Want to Be Like Jesus!" Display your poster in the classroom or in a hallway.

TRICKY TIPS

✱ If children are dipping their own papers, have them wear plastic gloves or sandwich bags on their hands. Be sure to have kids wash their hands afterward.

✱ Keep extra blueprint paper in a black bag and place it in the freezer to keep it cold and dark. The paper should last for several weeks.

Strong-Stander

eSPECIALly His

**OAL GETTER:**
This amazing trick helps kids realize that Jesus knows them by name.

**ERSES TO VIEW:**
John 10:1-5, 14-15

TRICKS OF THE TRADE:
You'll need a Bible, paper lunch sacks, a quarter, a dime, and enough nickels and pennies for each pair of children to have two coins.

The Dynamite Devotion

Set four different coins and a paper sack on a table near where you plan to stand. Gather children in front of you. Ask:

● **Have you ever met someone who knew your name before you told it to him or her? Explain.**

Say: **It would be pretty surprising to know everyone's name, especially in a crowd. Let's see if I can tell you someone's name without seeing that person. There are some coins on this table, and they have people's pictures on them.** Hold up the coins one at a time, and encourage kids to tell the name of each president pictured. Then choose a volunteer to stand by the coins.

Say: **Choose a coin, and hold it up for everyone but me to see. Then hold the coin tightly in your hand. I won't peek!** Pause for a moment as the volunteer chooses a coin and shows it to the children. Be sure the volunteer continues to hold the coin tightly during the following statements. Say: **You know the Bible tells us about someone who knows everyone's name and in fact *calls* them by name. Do you know who calls us by name?** Pause for responses, then say: **Jesus is the one who calls us by name! You see, Jesus is like a shepherd, and we are his sheep.**

Read aloud John 10:1-5, 14-15. Then say:

A good shepherd knows every single sheep in the flock, and the shepherd knows the name of every sheep, too. The Bible tells us that Jesus is the Good Shepherd, and he knows our names and everything about us. Even in a crowd, Jesus can pick us out! Now let's see if I can pick out the person you chose.

Without looking, instruct the volunteer to place all four coins in the paper sack. Then shake the sack a few times to mix up the coins. Reach into the sack and feel for the coin that's been warmed by the volunteer's hand. Pull out the coin, then say to the group, "Here is (first name of the president on the coin)." Have the volunteer confirm the coin as the one he or she chose.

Say: **Pretty neat trick, isn't it? But Jesus knows us and that's no trick!** Ask:

● **How does it feel to know that Jesus knows you?**

● **What difference does it make in your life knowing that Jesus knows everything about you?**

● **How can you get to know Jesus better?**

Explain how the trick works, then let children find partners. Hand each pair a paper sack and a nickel and a penny. Allow them to take turns practicing the trick. Encourage children to try this trick with their families and friends as they explain how Jesus knows and calls each of us by name.

Extra Excitement

● Let children do a coin collage by smoothing aluminum foil over various coins and rubbing them with their fingernails. The three-dimensional relief of the coins will appear on the foil!

● Invite younger children to play a game of Where's Abe? Let two children place pennies in plain sight around the room. Then let the rest of the class hunt for the coins. Each time a penny is found, a child must say, "Here's Abe!" Play until everyone's had a turn "hiding" coins.

TRICKY TIPS

✳ Make sure your partner holds the coin long enough for it to become warm!

✳ Use the penny trick for teaching the parable of the lost sheep or coin (Luke 15:3-7, 8-10), and for learning that there's only *one* God (Deuteronomy 5:7).

Up With the Lord!

GOAL GETTER:

Partners help each other make paper dolls "dance" as they discover how Jesus lifts even the saddest heart with joy.

VERSES TO VIEW:

Luke 24:50-52

TRICKS OF THE TRADE:

You'll need a Bible, plastic wrap, tracing paper, scissors, markers, and items made of wool (stocking caps, mittens, wool socks, or wool fabric scraps). You'll also need a photocopy of the "Dancing Doll" handout on page 116 for each child.

The Dynamite Devotion

Before this devotion, make the photocopies of the "Dancing Doll" handout from page 116, directly on tracing paper if possible. Cut one Dancing Doll from tracing paper. You may wish to use markers to decorate the doll. Then tear off a twelve-inch piece of plastic wrap.

Place the Dancing Doll, plastic wrap, and a wool item beside you. Have kids form pairs and sit with their partners. Say: **Turn to your partner and tell about a time you felt really down in the dumps or sad. Then tell your partner what made you feel better.** Allow time for partners to share their experiences.

Hold up the decorated Dancing Doll and say: **We've all experienced times when nothing seemed happy or good. Maybe your best friend was angry with you or it rained on your birthday picnic. Whatever the cause, you probably felt like flopping to the floor and not getting up!** Let the Dancing Doll flutter to the floor.

Hold the piece of plastic wrap about three inches above the Dancing Doll. Hold the wrap so it's very taut. Say: **When we're really down in the dumps, it's important to know that Jesus helps us feel happier. Let's see what the Bible says about how Jesus makes people happy. Jesus' disciples had been sad because Jesus had died. But they were joyful after he rose from the dead.**

Choose two volunteers. Have one volunteer read aloud Luke 24:50-52, and have the other rub the wool item back and forth across the plastic wrap. As static electricity is formed, the Dancing Doll will "stand up." When the doll is standing, stop rubbing wool on the plastic wrap. Move the plastic wrap gently back and forth, keeping it taut. The paper doll will appear to "dance."

Say: **See? When we think about and praise Jesus, we don't have to feel sad—we can jump for joy instead! Jesus turns our sadness to gladness in a snap.**

Hand each child a photocopy of the Dancing Doll. If there's time, invite partners to cut out the paper dolls and decorate them. Then hand each child a twelve-inch piece of plastic wrap. Encourage children to practice the Dancing Doll trick with each other then present the devotion to family and friends. Remind children to tell people that Jesus lifts our hearts with joy when we're feeling down.

Extra Excitement

● Demonstrate how to fold and cut out a string of old-fashioned paper dolls. Hand each child a section of paper dolls to decorate. Then encourage children to write words on the dolls to describe the way Jesus makes them feel, such as joyous, secure, hopeful, and loved. Display the paper dolls by letting them "dance" down hallways or around doors.

● Have more fun with static electricity. Have kids rub blown up balloons back and forth across their clothes, then hold the balloons next to their hair. You'll get plenty of giggles as kids' hair "rises" to the occasion. Point out how static electricity may raise paper dolls or hair, but that only Jesus can lift the saddest hearts and give them joy.

TRICKY TIPS

✳ Be sure to use 100 percent wool fabric. Other materials don't create enough static electricity for good results.

✳ Tracing paper is available at art and office supply stores.

GOAL GETTER:
This humorous devotion teaches kids that it's important to trust in God to help us accomplish difficult challenges.

VERSES TO VIEW:
Psalm 63:1-8

TRICKS OF THE TRADE:
You'll need a Bible and plastic spoons.

The Great Dangling Spoons Duel

The Dynamite Devotion

Be sure you have a spoon for each child in class. Have kids get into pairs or trios and ask:

● **What's the hardest thing you've ever done?**

● **How did you finally accomplish your task?**

Say: **It's not unusual to face big challenges and difficulties in our lives. In fact, I have a difficult challenge for you right now.** Hold up a plastic spoon. **Let's see if you can hang a spoon from the end of your nose while you're looking straight ahead.** Hand each child a plastic spoon, and allow time for them to try and accomplish this zany challenge.

After a few minutes, call time. Then say: **Pretty hard to do, isn't it? But so are most difficult challenges. Who can we turn to for help when we face tough things in our lives? Let's find the answer to this challenging question in the Bible.** Have a volunteer read aloud Psalm 63:1-8. Then say: **God can help us accomplish even our most difficult tasks. When we pray and ask for God's help, he gives us answers and ways to do what we're challenged to do.** Lick your finger and rub it on the tip of your nose. Then breathe heavily on the bowl of the spoon. Wait a moment, then hang the tip of the spoon on your nose. Let the spoon balance in place for several seconds, then remove it.

Say: **You see, with the right help, you can meet any challenge—and God provides help to face the most difficult challenges in our lives.** Ask:

● **How can you rely on God's help with challenges you're facing today?**

Say: **This was a cool trick, but relying on God's help isn't a trick at all. Just remember to hang onto God for help!** Hang the spoon on your nose for another second or two.

Explain how the trick works, then let children practice the trick with their plastic spoons. Encourage children to challenge their families and friends with this nifty trick as they explain how hanging onto God's help can see us through our most difficult challenges.

Extra Excitement

● Younger kids will love decorating their plastic spoons with colorful markers to make spoon people. Encourage kids to use their spoon people to perform this devotion for their families.

● Invite kids to create unusual challenges, such as balancing a book on their little fingers or closing their eyes as they hop across the room on one foot. When everyone's had a turn to challenge the group, talk about challenges Jesus can help with in real life.

TRICKY TIPS

✱ Metal spoons work well for this devotion, so encourage kids to perform this trick at the table to make a great mealtime devotion.

✱ Practice this trick several times to get the "hang" of it!

Communication— Cooperation

The Dynamite Devotion

This is a great devotion for two kids to present as a team. Designate one partner as the Counter and the other as the Placer. This trick involves quick counting and sly movements, so be sure to have the partners practice their trick several times to get the hang of it!

Gather kids on the floor. Have the Placer hold the spoons, knives, and forks. (Shh, keep a secret! Don't let on who is the Counter!) Have the Placer say: **Let's play a tricky game. I'll place some of this plastic tableware on the floor, then ask you what number I made. Call out the number you think I made with the tableware.**

The Placer lays down any combination of forks, spoons, and knives on the floor. The tableware can be laid in a pattern, overlapping, or at random. Then the Placer thinks of a number between one and ten, and slyly lays that number of fingers on his or her knees. The Placer asks, "What number did I make?" Counter, this is your cue to quickly add the number of fingers your partner is showing. Let a few kids tell their ideas, then call out the correct number, but don't tell how you got it . . . yet. Repeat the trick a few more times to see if anyone catches on, then explain how the Counter always knew the right number. Ask:

- **How did the Placer serve the Counter?**
- **How did the Counter serve the Placer?**
- **What was it like when the Counter always knew the right number?**

Say: **This neat little trick is a good example of serving each other. Let's see what the Bible says about serving.** Read aloud Luke 22:26-27. Then ask:

- **Why do you think God wants us to serve each other?**

Say: **When we serve and help others, we're better able to serve God. Now tell me once more what number I make.** Repeat the trick, and have kids tell the correct number.

Have kids form pairs, and hand each pair a set of plastic tableware. Let kids practice being Placers and Counters as they perform this trick. Encourage kids to find a partner and present this duo-devotion to family and friends. Remind kids to tell their audience about the importance of communicating and cooperating with others to serve God.

Extra Excitement

● Get communicating and start cooperating with each other as you make "Snappy Snack-Sacks" for elderly neighbors or shut-ins. Have kids form the following groups: the Artists, who decorate paper lunch sacks; the Happy-Apples, who place an apple in each sack; the Cheery-Cheesers, who put packages of string cheese into the sacks; and the Handy-Candies, who drop Hershey's Kisses into the snack sacks. Let kids deliver the sacks to elderly neighbors or shut-ins to brighten their day.

TRICKY TIPS

✳ The key to this devotional trick is communication! Be sure partners practice their techniques before presenting this devotion.

✳ Use books, paper scraps, or other items in place of plastic tableware.

The Baffling Boat Race

GOAL GETTER:
This devotion isn't all wet—it teaches kids what running the "good race" is all about.

VERSES TO VIEW:
1 Corinthians 9:24-27

TRICKS OF THE TRADE:
You'll need a Bible, the boat pattern on page 93, index cards, a dishpan of water, liquid dish detergent, scissors, paper cups, a plastic tablecloth, and toothpicks.

The Dynamite Devotion

Before this devotion, make several boats using index cards and the boat pattern on page 93. Fill a dishpan with water, and set it on the floor on a plastic tablecloth. Place toothpicks, paper boats, and a paper cup containing dish detergent by the dishpan.

Say: **I love races, and I love boats.** Hold up the paper boat. **I have a very special boat here. Oh, I know it looks ordinary, but it's really a special boat that wins races. Who wants to choose a boat and race?** Have a volunteer pick a paper boat. **We'll put our boats in the water, then have everyone count to three and say "go!" You can blow on your boat or fan it or whatever, and I'll do the same. We'll race to the other side of the dishpan. Ready?**

Put your boats in the water. Have kids count to three and say, "go!" Quickly dip your toothpick in dish detergent, and carefully drop the detergent from the toothpick into the triangular hole in the boat. It should zoom ahead! Continue dropping detergent from the toothpick until your boat reaches the finish line. Challenge other volunteers to race. Then ask:

● **How did my boat go so fast?**
● **Was this a fair race? Explain.**

Say: **Some races don't seem fair. In fact, many races aren't even worth competing in. This boat race was a little silly, but the Bible tells us about one race that's very serious—and it's for keeps! Let's read about that race.**

Have a volunteer read aloud 1 Corinthians 9:24-27. Then ask:

- **What kind of race is the Bible talking about?**
- **What makes this race important?**

Say: **I won the boat races because I knew what things would help me win. Soap was just the right "equipment" to help me win boat races.**

- **What "equipment" do we need to help us win the "good race"?**
- **How does Jesus help us win the good race?**

Say: **Running the good race is important, and so is winning it. With the right equipment, we can have the victory! Remember, this is one race that Jesus wants us to win.**

Give each child an index card. Then have kids form pairs and create their own boats. Invite kids to take turns racing their boats using liquid soap and toothpicks. Challenge kids to make several boats and invite family members or friends to race. Remind kids to explain about the "good race" and how Jesus helps us win it.

Extra Excitement

- Host an outdoor Track and Field Day with your class. String a crepe paper finish line at one end of the playing area, and use a rope to designate a starting line at the opposite end. Let kids race in events such as the Crazy Crab Walk, the Tiptoe Mile, and the Partner Bunny-Hop. Offer cool apple juice to energize thirsty racers, and award everyone a graham cracker "trophy" when you've completed all of the events.

- Let kids make beautiful poster board boats with markers, sequins, and glitter glue. Cover the boats with clear self-adhesive paper to make them last. Use the boats to race with, or suggest that kids use them as Bible bookmarks to remind them of the "good race."

TRICKY TIPS

✳ Wash and dry the dishpan between boat races for the best results.

God's Special One

GOAL GETTER:

This classic card trick teaches kids that God knows us because he created each of us special.

VERSE TO VIEW:

Psalm 139:14

TRICKS OF THE TRADE:

You'll need a Bible and several decks of playing cards with pictures on the backs of the cards. Old Maid and animal rummy cards will work for this devotion if you'd rather not use traditional playing cards.

The Dynamite Devotion

Arrange the playing cards in a stack with the pictures on the backs all facing the same direction. Gather kids in a group, and ask:

● **Who's the most special person you know?**

● **What makes someone special?**

Say: **We know lots of people from our families, school, church, and neighborhoods. You probably even "know" some people without knowing their names, like the man at the grocery store or the neat lady at the pharmacy. Let's pretend these cards are a big crowd of people. Can you pick a special one out of the crowd?**

Hold the cards in a fan, face down. Choose a child to pick a card and show it to the rest of the audience, but not to you. As the child displays the card, quickly (and slyly!) turn the deck of cards around.

Then say: **Now let's hide the special one in this crowd.** Take the card and, without peeking at it, slide the card into the deck. Be sure the back of the card is facing in the opposite direction from the rest of the deck.

Say: **Before we try to find the special card, let's see what the Bible tells us about being God's special ones.** Read aloud Psalm 139:14. Then ask:

● **Who does God consider special?**

● **Why does God think we're special?**

● **If God created each of us, is anyone *not* valued in his eyes? Explain.**

Slowly lay the cards face down, one at a time. Stop when you get to the card that's facing in the opposite direction. As you lay down cards, say: **God made each of us, and he knows us better than anyone. In fact, we're so special to God, he can pick us out of a huge crowd!** Turn over the card that was upside down and show it to the kids. **Now *that's* a great feat, but it's no trick to**

God. He made us and we're all special!

Explain how the trick is done, then let kids get into pairs and take turns picking and finding cards. Encourage kids to present this simple but super devotion to their families and friends. Remind kids to tell their audiences how special they are in God's eyes.

Extra Excitement

● Have kids make their own sets of Me Cards. Give each child ten index cards, and invite kids to use markers or crayons to draw pictures and shapes that tell about themselves. When everyone is finished, have them form pairs and exchange cards. Encourage partners to tell each other about their cards. Remind them that each of us is special to God.

● Play a quick game of Special Mystery Person. Have kids close their eyes, then gently tap a child on the head. This is the person who the others will try to identify. Have children open their eyes and ask questions about the "mystery" person. Ask questions such as "Is this person a boy or a girl?" or "What color eyes does this person have?" Challenge kids to identify the mystery person with fewer than five questions.

TRICKY TIPS

✳ Be sure the cards are face down with all pictures in the same direction before starting this devotion.

✳ Make certain that you replace the chosen card in the opposite direction of the other cards in the deck.

VERSE TO VIEW:
Joshua 1:9

TRICKS OF THE TRADE:
You'll need a Bible, a men's handkerchief or a small silk scarf, and string.

1

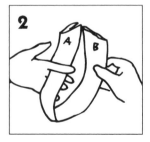

2

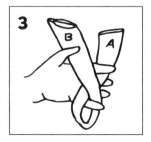

3

The Disappearing Knot

The Dynamite Devotion

This eye-catching trick depends a bit on practice. Be sure you're comfortable with how to tie and release the knot before presenting this devotion. Follow the diagrams and directions below for tying the knot. Bring end B over end A. Poke B behind A and pull end B to the front.

Gather kids around you, and choose one child to be your partner to help untie your special knot. Ask your audience:

● **When's a time you felt scared?**
● **How is fear like a knot?**

Hold up the handkerchief and tie the special knot as you say: **Fear is like a knot. It ties us up in worry and keeps us from feeling happy. Fear also stops us from freely serving God.** Look at the knot and at your partner. Say: **Wow! This is a nasty knot—just like a big knot of fear. How can we untie the knots we feel inside?** Allow kids to tell their ideas.

Say: **We can ask God's help in untying those stubborn knots of fear. We can pray, then trust God to help us. Remember, no fear is too big or too hard for God to untie. God can do anything!** Hold the knot under your partner's chin, and ask him or her to blow on it. As your partner blows on the knot, gently tug the ends and the knot will disappear. Voilà! Then say: **Untying a knot is just that simple for God. Let's read what the Bible tells us about trusting God to take away our fears.**

Ask a volunteer to read aloud Joshua 1:9. Then ask:

● **Why is it wise to trust God to help with our problems?**

● **How can we learn to trust God?**

Say: **It's one thing to ask God's help with our fears, but we also need to trust God's answers. No knots of fear are too big for God to handle.** Tie your special knot once more. **And our prayers and trust in God will untie every knot!** Blow on the knot and pull the ends to release it.

Hand each child a piece of string. Demonstrate and explain how to tie and release the special slip knot. Then let kids practice tying and untying knots with partners. Encourage kids to present this cool devotion to their families and friends. Remind them to tell their audiences that God can untie our knots of fear if we just trust him.

Extra Excitement

● Let kids tie love knots to remind them of our love, faith, and trust in God. Hand each child a twenty-four-inch length of jute rope. Help them tie a series of three knots down the length of the rope. Have kids fringe the ends of the rope, then tie ribbon loops to the top end of each rope. Encourage the kids to hang their love knots on a door or wall. Remind kids that when we tie knots of love, faith, and trust with God's help, they can't be untied or destroyed.

● Younger kids will enjoy singing "T-R-U-S-T" to the tune of "Old MacDonald Had a Farm," and they'll learn how to spell this important word too!

God wants us to love and trust.
T-R-U-S-T!
It's a gift to God from us.
T-R-U-S-T!
I can trust, 'cuz I know,
Love from God makes my trust grow.
God wants us to love and trust.
T-R-U-S-T!

TRICKY TIPS

✳ Men's neckties work well for tying disappearing knots. Consider shopping thrift stores to purchase a necktie for each child in class to use for this devotion.

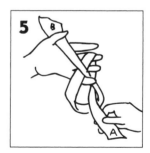

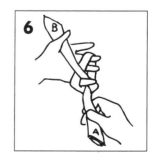

The Impossible Paper Lift

OAL GETTER:
This crazy trick will astound kids as they learn how prayer "lifts" away things that keep us from God.

ERSES TO VIEW:
James 4:7-8

RICKS OF THE TRADE:
You'll need a Bible, newspapers, a yardstick, a marker, and an index card.

The Dynamite Devotion

Before this devotion, write the word "God" on an index card. Stack several layers of newspaper on a rectangular or square table. Position the papers so the long edges run along the edge of the table. Slip the yardstick under the center of the newspapers so half of it sticks out from the edge of the table. Gather kids around the table. Hold up the index card and ask:

● **What things keep us from God?**

Say: **Things such as jealousy, meanness, lying, and saying bad words keep us from being close to God. When we have negative thoughts and words, it's almost as if God's love becomes buried.** Slide the index card under the newspapers. **And it's not as easy as it looks to uncover the mess! Who would like to try?**

Choose one person at a time to attempt lifting the newspapers by slapping the yardstick in a single, swift downward motion. The papers shouldn't budge! After a few children try to remove the papers, say: **It's not as simple as it looks, is it? So how** *do* **we rid ourselves of things such as jealousy and mean words?** Let kids offer their ideas, then read aloud James 4:7-8.

Say: **Drawing close to God is the answer! When we pray and ask God to help us grow closer to him, negative things such as dishonesty, jealousy, and unkindness lift from our lives.** Slowly push down on the yardstick. The newspapers should easily lift to reveal the index card. **Drawing close to God lifts obstacles that keep us from following God faithfully.**

Explain how the trick is done. Then let kids get into pairs and take turns swiftly slapping the yardstick, then gently pushing downward on it to reveal the index card. Encourage kids to present this simply super devotion to their families and friends. Remind kids to tell their audiences how prayer lifts away bad things that keep us from God.

Extra Excitement

● Invite kids to participate in a cooperative weight lifting challenge. Form groups of three, and lift things such as pencils, wastebaskets, tables, chairs, or stacks of books. Have kids lift a willing adult for the grand finale. Position the adult in a chair and have the kids lift the chair one inch off the ground. Point out how many hands make lifting easier, just as many hands in prayer lift the heaviest burdens.

● Young children will enjoy making prayer-power barbells. Help each child blow up and tie off two balloons of the same size. Let each person tape a plastic drinking straw between the balloons to make a barbell. Help kids each write the word "Prayer" on one balloon, and the word "Power" on the other balloon. Challenge children to lift their prayer-power barbells after each time they pray.

TRICKY TIPS

✳ Be sure to slap down on the yardstick with a single, swift motion.

✳ Keep the newspapers in a pile atop the index card and the yardstick.

A Super-Standing Challenge

GOAL GETTER:
This surprising devotion challenges kids to stand on the firm foundation of Jesus.

VERSE TO VIEW:
1 Corinthians 3:11

TRICKS OF THE TRADE:
You'll need a sheet of newsprint or poster board, a marker, tape, a Bible, and access to a wall.

The Dynamite Devotion

Before this devotion, write the name "JESUS" on a large sheet of newsprint or poster board. Tape the paper to a wall.

Gather kids near the wall, and have them find partners. Say: **I wonder if you and your partner know what kind of ground is the sturdiest to stand on. See if you can balance on one foot.** Pause. **Now balance on the tiptoes of one foot.** Pause. **OK, let's see you hop up and down, then sit down.**

When everyone is sitting, ask:

● **Are you standing firm when balancing on one foot? Explain.**

● **What's it like to be standing on shaky or unlevel ground?**

● **What happens if we stand on rocky ground or can't balance ourselves?**

Say: **We often find ourselves standing on shaky ground in life. We may not be sure of the right thing to do or say. We may not understand why we're supposed to do something. It's kind of scary when we're feeling unbalanced and like we might fall. So what's the best way to stand firm? Look at the wall. What does it say?** Have someone read aloud Jesus' name.

Then say: **Let's see if leaning on Jesus helps us stand firm. Place your right feet and cheeks against the wall. Now try to lift your left foot off the ground. Can you do it?** Pause for responses. Say: **You can't get unbalanced or fall down—in fact, when we lean on Jesus for support, he won't let our feet slip at all! Let's sit down and hear**

what the Bible says about standing on the firm foundation of Jesus.

Ask two volunteers to read aloud 1 Corinthians 3:11. Then ask:

● **What's the best foundation to stand on? Why?**

● **Why won't Jesus let us fall when we're leaning on him?**

● **How can we lean on Jesus?**

Say: **Stand up and put your right feet and cheeks against the wall again.** Have kids try once more to lift their left feet off the ground or hop on their right feet. Then say: **As long as we're leaning on Jesus, we can't fall and won't stumble. Jesus is the firm foundation we stand on.**

Encourage kids to challenge their families and friends to this "standing duel." Have them present the devotion and explain that Jesus is the firm foundation we always want to stand on.

Extra Excitement

● Let kids sculpt "Standing on the Rock of Jesus" sculptures. Hand each child a two-foot length of aluminum foil, and have them shape the foil into a standing figure. Then give each child a large stone or small brick on which to mount their creations. Use florists' clay to stick figures to the stone. You may wish to have kids title their sculptures such as "Standing Strong" or "Firm on the Foundation of Jesus."

● Play an action game to get the wiggles out. Tear "rocks" from brown paper grocery sacks. Scatter the paper rocks around the floor, and tape them in place. Choose one child to be "It," and have him or her hop to tag others. Instruct kids that they too must hop, and that safe areas are the paper rocks. Tell kids that they may stand on paper rocks to avoid being tagged. When someone is tagged, start a new game and vary the mode of "travel" such as walking backward or heel-to-toe.

TRICKY TIPS

✳ Trees, doors, fences, and other solid structures work as well as walls for this devotion.

Can't Hide That Heart

GOAL GETTER: In this devotion, kids learn that we can't hide our feelings from God.

VERSE TO VIEW: 1 Samuel 16:7

TRICKS OF THE TRADE: You'll need a Bible, red construction paper, scissors, and several clear drinking glasses filled with water.

The Dynamite Devotion

Before this devotion, cut one-inch hearts from red construction paper. Cut a paper heart for every two or three kids.

Direct kids to form pairs or trios. Give each group of kids a paper heart and a glass of water. Ask:

● **When have you tried to hide your feelings about something or someone?**

● **Did anyone know you weren't being honest about your feelings? Explain.**

Say: **Sometimes we say we like something when we really don't. Or we may pretend to be happy when we're really hurting inside. It's easy to think that no one sees inside us and can tell when we're not true to the feelings in our hearts.**

Can you see your paper heart and glass of water? Hold up a paper heart and point to a glass of water. **People see what's on the outside of others. They can't see what's inside our hearts. Sometimes it's easy to hide ourselves from other people.** Have kids place their glasses on top of the paper hearts. **Look! The hearts have disappeared from sight!** Invite your audience to look through the *sides* of the drinking glasses. The paper hearts should "disappear." **We may think we've hidden our thoughts and feelings—but they're still there. They haven't really disappeared. Did you know there *is* someone who sees our hearts and what's inside them? Who do you think that is?** Pause for kids to tell their ideas.

Say: **God always knows what's inside us—even when we try to hide it! Let's read about how God sees us.** Have a volunteer read aloud 1 Samuel 16:7. Then ask:

● **How does God look at us?**

● **Can we ever hide our feelings from God? Explain.**

● **How does it feel to know that God sees all our thoughts and feelings?**

Say: **Look through your glass once more.** This time, have kids look down through the top of the glass. **Do you see the heart? This is how God sees us. Even when we think we've hidden ourselves** (peek through the side of the glass), **God sees our hearts!** Look down through the top of the glass.

Encourage kids to present this simple devotion to their families and friends. Remind kids to tell others that God always knows our thoughts and feelings because he looks *inside* our hearts.

Extra Excitement

● Let kids make "Inside My Heart" pictures. Have kids cut various sizes and colors of construction paper hearts. Show kids how to glue the top portions of the hearts to a sheet of paper to make "peekaboo" flaps. Then invite kids to draw pictures or write words under the hearts to describe their inner feelings, thoughts, hopes, and dreams. If there's time, let kids form trios and tell about their pictures.

● Young children will enjoy a game of Hidden Hearts. Have kids sit in a circle, and choose two children to sit in the center. Pass two small candy or paper hearts around the circle. Tell kids to pass the hearts sneakily so the center people won't know where the hearts are. Lead the children in saying, "God looks at our hearts—not our outsides." When you've repeated the sentence, stop passing the hearts. Let the children in the center each have two guesses to find someone with a heart. Have them exchange places with the players holding the hearts.

TRICKY TIPS

✱ Be sure to have your audience look through the side of the drinking glass, level with the table.

✱ If you don't have red construction paper, draw a heart on white paper with a red marker.

Glued to Your Chair?

GOAL GETTER:

This crazy devotion challenges kids to get up and go for God.

VERSE TO VIEW:

Luke 9:23

TRICKS OF THE TRADE:

You'll need a straight chair for each child and a Bible.

The Dynamite Devotion

Arrange the chairs in a circle, and invite each person to stand by a chair. Say: **Let's play a little game. I'll give you some directions to follow. Your job is to listen carefully, then follow my directions. Ready? Sit straight in your chair, and put your back against the back of the chair.** Pause. **Place your feet flat on the floor.** Pause. **Put your fingers on your nose.** Pause for responses. **Nod your heads yes if you love God.** Pause. **Wink your eyes three times.** Pause. **Now cross your arms and place your hands on your shoulders to show how much you love Jesus.** Pause. **Hold your hands on your shoulders, and without bending forward, stand straight up to show you're ready to serve God!** No one will be able to stand if kids' backs are straight in the chairs and their feet are on the floor.

After a moment say: **Well. I see you're still sitting in your chairs. What can be wrong? You know, many people do just the same thing when God calls them to serve. They stay stuck in one place and don't move!** Ask:

● **Why does God call us to follow him?**

● **What keeps people from obeying God's call?**

Say: **Staying stuck in one place when God wants us to get up and go can be pretty awful. God wants us ready and willing to follow him— any time, any place. Let's read what the Bible says about being ready to serve.**

Have a volunteer read aloud Luke 9:23. Then ask:

● **How can we be ready to follow when God calls?**

● **What role does faith play in getting us "unstuck"?**

● **How can you follow God this week?**

Say: **When God calls us, we want to get up and go forward. Now lean forward in your chairs and stand up to show you're ready to go for God.** This time everyone should be able to stand up. Encourage kids to share this devotion with their families and friends. Remind them to tell others that we don't want to be stuck when God calls—we want to get up and go for God!

Extra Excitement

● Play a game similar to the old favorite Red Light, Green Light. Have kids sit at one end of the room. When you say, "Get up and go-two," have kids pop up and take two giant steps forward, then sit down again. Vary the number you call out, and play until everyone reaches the opposite end of the room. For a twist, have kids lie down instead of sit.

TRICKY TIPS

✳ Be sure everyone's backs are *straight* against the backs of their chairs, and they keep their backs straight when trying to stand.

OAL GETTER:
In this great bit of daring, kids will learn about giving to God.

ERSES TO VIEW:
2 Corinthians 9:7-8

RICKS OF THE TRADE:
You'll need a penny for each child and a Bible.

No Penny-Pinching!

The Dynamite Devotion

Have kids form pairs, and hand each pair a penny. Ask:

● **When have you given something to help another person? How did it feel?**

● **When have you not wanted to give away something you owned? How did you feel?**

Say: **Let's see how good you are at giving away money. Choose one partner to be the Holder and one to be the Placer. Holders, place the tips of your ring fingers together. Now fold your other fingers so the knuckles touch. Placers, slide the penny between the tips of the Holders' ring fingers.** Pause to give kids time to follow your directions.

Say: **I see a lot of pennies that can be used to help people who need them. Holders, donate your pennies by dropping them on the floor. Don't slide your fingers, just let the pennies drop.** No pennies will clatter to the floor! Say: **Oh my! No one is donating any money. It seems as though everyone is pinching pennies to keep what they have. Sometimes this same thing happens when we know someone needs our help. We can't seem to let go of money, talents, or time to help others.** Have kids set their pennies down, then ask:

● **Do you think God wants us to give our money, talents, and time to help others? Why or why not?**

Say: **Let's read what the Bible says about giving freely.** Have a volunteer read aloud 2 Corinthians 9:7-8. Then ask:

● **What does God promise if we give to others?**

● **What are ways we can give to help others?**

● **How does giving help our faith grow?**

● In what ways can you give to others this week?

Say: **When we say someone is pinching pennies, we mean they don't want to give up even a little of their money. But God tells us to give freely and not pinch pennies. In fact, God promises great blessings if we give freely of our time, money, and talents!**

Let kids switch roles of Holder and Placer and try the trick again. Give each child a penny to take home. Encourage kids to present this devotion to their families and friends. Remind them to tell their audiences that God wants us to give freely to help others, then he'll bless us.

Extra Excitement

● Decorate "God's Piggy Banks." Give each child a container, such as a small box, empty yogurt container, or margarine tub, to decorate with markers and bits of construction paper. Help each child cut a slot in the bank to slide coins through. Encourage kids to give "a penny a day" to their banks, then collect the money at the end of the month to donate to a local service organization or a foreign mission your church supports.

● Get your kids involved in a service project such as making cookies for nursing home residents or hosting a blanket drive for elderly people in the wintertime. Wrap your donations in bright gift wrap and bows. Emphasize that giving goes beyond money—it means giving of ourselves and our time as well!

TRICKY TIPS

✳ This devotion will work with any coin or paper bill.

✳ Consider letting a child present this devotion to the adults if a sermon is given on the topic of stewardship or giving. Have all the adults participate using partners and coins.

Sink or Swim

GOAL GETTER:
In this amazing devotion, kids learn that honesty keeps them afloat.

VERSE TO VIEW:
Proverbs 12:22

TRICKS OF THE TRADE:
You'll need a Bible, a raw potato, a knife, a pencil, a permanent marker, salt, a measuring cup, and a clear glass of water.

The Dynamite Devotion

This is a perfect devotion for two kids to present. It takes a bit of preparation, but it's worth it! Let one partner prepare the pitcher and potato, and the other tell the accompanying story. Have the person preparing the pitcher and potato follow these steps:

1. Cut the tip from a raw potato. Use a permanent marker to draw a face on the small piece of potato.

2. The night before the devotion, fill a clear drinking glass half full of very hot water. Stir one-half cup of salt into the water. Place the piece of potato into the glass. If it floats, you have enough salt. If the potato sinks, add salt until it floats. Remove the potato and set it aside. Let the saltwater cool overnight. The water will be cloudy at first, but will clear up.

3. Just before the devotion, pour fresh tap water very, *very* slowly down the side of the glass until it's nearly full. Be careful not to let the fresh water mix with the saltwater. This is tricky, but you can do it! When you're done, you'll have what looks like a glass of ordinary water. Now you're set to begin.

Place the glass of water and the potato on a table. Set a pencil next to the glass, then gather kids near the table. Have the "storyteller" hold up the potato and say:

I have a story to tell you about Spud. When you hear Spud lie, cover your ears and shake your head.

Spud wanted to swim one real hot day (hold up potato),

but his parents said, "No, Spud, not today."

Spud smiled and said, "OK, I'll obey," (make potato "nod")

and headed for the swimming hole right away.

Fresh water

Saltwater

Saltwater mixes with fresh water

Spud saw the water shimmering bright (make pota-to "hop");

he thought he could swim—

but Spud wasn't right! (Place potato in water.)

Spud found himself in a terrible spot (potato will sink);

It was sink or swim until he cried, "Stop!" (Potato will stop sinking when it hits the saltwater.)

Spud knew that his lie had got him in deep;

He found that the TRUTH was the best thing to keep!

So Spud prayed to God to keep him afloat (stir water with pencil),

And popped to the top like a po-ta-to boat! (Potato will float to the top as saltwater and fresh water mix.)

Spud decided right then to be honest and true,

And thanked God for honesty and his love, too!

When you're through with the story, ask:

● **What happens when we're dishonest?**

● **Why do you think God wants honesty?**

● **How can you have more honesty in your life?**

Read aloud Proverbs 12:22. Then say: **Spud learned that telling lies makes us heavy and feels as if we're sinking. But when we ask God's help in being honest, we stay afloat. God wants us to be truthful and true in all we say and all we do!**

Explain to kids how to prepare the special water and potato. Be sure to point out that a potato sinks in fresh water, but will stop sinking when it reaches the saltwater. When you mix the saltwater and fresh water, the potato will float. Challenge kids to present this devotion to their families and friends. Remind them to tell their audiences that God wants us to be honest in all we say and do.

Extra Excitement

● Play the age old favorite: Hot Potato. Each time a player tosses a potato, have him or her tell one true thing about God, such as "God loves us" or "God wants us to be honest."

TRICKY TIPS

✱ If you don't want to wait overnight for the saltwater to cool, you can prepare a glass of saltwater and fresh water. The saltwater will be cloudy, but the devotion will work just fine.

No Strings Attached

A.

— string

B.

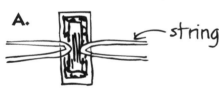

← paper clip
← string
— fold over paper

C.

The Dynamite Devotion

This devotion is great for partners to perform, but it takes a bit of practice. Be sure you're comfortable with how to prepare the string and paper clip before presenting this devotion. Follow the illustrated directions for attaching the string and paper clip to the "Gift of Grace" handout.

Cut two twelve-inch pieces of string, and loop each piece in half. Lay the loops on the "Gift of Grace" paper so they meet in the center. (See diagram A.) Then fold the "Gift of Grace" paper end-over-end around the loops and attach a paper clip at the top. (See diagram B.)

Gather kids and set the "Gift of Grace" paper with the strings attached beside you. Ask:

- **When's a time you received a gift?**
- **How did it feel to get a gift?**
- **Why do people give gifts?**
- **How does it feel to give a special gift to someone?**

Partner 1: **Giving gifts shows our love—and it's fun! One neat thing about gifts is that they're given freely. That means there are no strings attached—they're free.** Carefully hold up the paper on the strings. Lift one string from each side of the paper and carefully tie the strings in a knot. (See diagram C.)

Partner 2: **But sometimes there *are* strings attached. We may give gifts but want something in return, such as giving a teacher a shiny apple and hoping for a good grade or helping mom with the dishes and hoping for extra money. Those aren't free gifts. In fact, they're not really gifts at all.**

Partner 1: **God gives us many different gifts. What are some of those gifts?** Allow time for kids to tell their ideas. Say: **God gives us lots of gifts, but the best gift he gives us is the gift of grace. Grace means we don't deserve to be loved or forgiven, but God gives us these things anyway. Watch what happens when God gives us this special gift.**

Each partner takes hold of the strings on either side of the paper. Have them give the strings a tug, and the paper should come free of the knotted string.

Partner 2: **See? God's gift has no strings attached!**

Partner 1: **God's gift of grace is free! Now let's read what it says.**

Have a volunteer read aloud Ephesians 2:8-9 from the "Gift of Grace" paper. Then invite kids to form pairs, and give each child two pieces of string, a paper clip, and a "Gift of Grace" handout. Explain how to attach the strings and paper clip to the paper and knot the strings. Let partners each pull the strings to release the paper. Encourage kids to present this devotion to their families and friends. Remind kids to tell their audiences that God's gift of grace is free—no strings attached!

Extra Excitement

● Make Gift of Grace gift boxes and bags to share with another class. Set out boxes, paper lunch bags, gift wrap, bows, and tape. Invite kids to decorate gift boxes and bags. Then place a "Gift of Grace" handout and a few Hershey's Kisses inside each gift. Be sure there's a box or bag for each child in the class you plan to visit. Let kids personally distribute their special deliveries.

● Brainstorm a class "Gift List" of all the things they could give as gifts. Be sure to include things such as a smile, a helping hand, a word of encouragement, a hand-drawn picture, and a cheery phone call. Talk about how gifts don't have to cost money—they just need to be given freely and with love. Then challenge kids to choose one "gift" from the list to give to someone that week. Leave the list on the wall and let kids tell about their gift-giving the following week.

TRICKY TIPS

✳ This is a great visual to use with lessons on tithing, stewardship, and giving to others even when we're tempted to hold onto what we have.

GOAL GETTER:
This eye-catching devotion teaches kids that people in God's family are locked together in his love.

VERSES TO VIEW:
Philippians 2:1-2

TRICKS OF THE TRADE:
You'll need a Bible, scissors, tape, and gift wrap in a heart pattern.

Locked in God's Love

The Dynamite Devotion

This pair-share devotion is best suited for older kids who are experienced with scissors.

Before this devotion, prepare a Möbius loop by cutting a three-inch by two-foot strip of gift wrap. Give the strip one twist, then tape the ends together front to back. Be sure the ends are covered with tape on both sides. Now poke the scissors through the center strip of the Möbius circle and cut around the circle to your starting place. You'll have a very large loop when finished.

Set the Möbius loop, scissors, and the Bible on a table. Gather kids and ask:

● **Who are the people in your family? in God's family?**

● **How are family members alike? different?**

Partner 1: **Our family members are different, but the members of God's family are all alike in one special way: They love and are loved by the same father who is God. It's like we're all in one big family.** Hold up the Möbius circle.

Partner 2: **God's love surrounds us, and he is at the center of this big circle of love. But what roles do each of us have in this special family? See if you can name some while we cut this circle to show you more about God's family.**

Encourage kids to name roles such as teachers, helpers, or encouragers. As you talk, poke the scissors through the center of the paper circle and cut around the middle. Have one partner cut while the other partner holds the circle and unwinds the paper strip. When you're finished cutting, hold up the strip.

Partner 1: **Look at the loop! There are now two loops locked together. See how each member of God's family has a special role and is still locked in God's love? Let's read what the Bible says about God's family, then we'll**

Turn one end once and tape

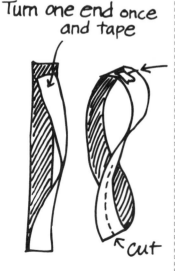

cut

see what happens to our circle of love.

Have a volunteer read aloud Philippians 2:1-2 as you cut down the centers of both loops. When you're finished cutting, have both partners each hold two circles.

Partner 2: **Wow! God's family keeps getting bigger, and yet we're all still locked in God's love. It's neat the way we're each separate and unique, yet held together by God's love.**

Partner 1: **When we're part of God's family, the circle of love grows. Each of us has our own special place in his family—and we're all joined to our Father with love!**

Have kids form pairs, and give scissors, tape, and gift wrap to each pair. Demonstrate how to prepare a Möbius circle, then explain how to cut the circles to make them interlock. Encourage kids to share this extraordinary devotion with their families and friends. Remind kids to tell others that when we're part of God's family, we're locked in God's love.

Extra Excitement

● Challenge pairs of older kids to see how many circles they can create from a four-inch by three-foot Möbius circle. Let kids count their circles and think of people they know who belong to God's family as well as others they could invite to be part of God's family.

● Let younger children make smiley faces on a large sheet of butcher paper or poster board. Then invite kids to dip raw potato halves in thinned tempera paint and stamp over the faces to make "people." Let kids write their own names below the faces, then title the cooperative poster "We're Happy to Be Part of God's Family." Display the cheery poster in a church hallway to bring everyone a smile.

TRICKY TIPS

✳ If you can't find heart-pattern gift wrap, any three-inch by two-foot strip of thin paper will work.

✳ Use sharp-tipped scissors for the best cutting results.

The Grand Finale: Set Me Free!

GOAL GETTER:

This eye-popping devotion teaches kids how to be free of bad things in their lives and live freely as Christians.

VERSES TO VIEW:

John 8:31-32

TRICKS OF THE TRADE:

You'll need a Bible, a handkerchief or scarf, several rolls of mint Life Savers candies, string cut in two-foot lengths, and paper towels.

The Dynamite Devotion

This devotion takes practice and a bit of preparation, but has dramatic results!

Before the devotion, bite a mint Life Savers candy in half. Wet the ends of the candy ring, and hold them together until they're dry. Now the ring will crack easily and silently during the devotion.

Place the handkerchief over a whole Life Savers candy on a table. Don't let your audience see the whole candy ring! Have Partner 1 hold the string by each end. Partner 2 can hold the "mended" candy ring.

Partner 2: **What are things that draw us away from God?** Allow kids to share their ideas. Mention things such as bad music, mean words, hanging out with the wrong kind of friends, and cheating.

Partner 1: **Many things draw us away from God and keep us trapped. It's almost as if we're chained to those bad things.** Have Partner 2 thread the mended candy ring onto the string. Be sure the string is stretched between the hands of Partner 1.

Partner 2: **When we're tied to bad things, how can we get free to follow God? Let's see what the Bible says about being set free.** Have a volunteer read aloud John 8:31-32. As the passage is being read, have Partner 2 slide the handkerchief and the whole candy ring off the

table, being careful to keep the candy hidden. After the Scripture is read, ask:

● **What are ways to free ourselves of bad things that keep us from following God?**

Have Partner 2 cover the candy ring on the string with the handkerchief, and say: **When we trust in God and obey what God wants us to do, we get rid of bad things, and we're free!** Slide both hands under the handkerchief and quickly break the ring on the string. Then pull away the handkerchief, hiding the broken ring in the fabric. Hold up the whole candy ring. Your audience will think it's the one that was on the string!

Partner 1: **Wow! We're free to follow God and live as he wants us to live.**

Partner 2: **And when we're free, we can serve others and spread God's message to everyone so they can be free too.**

Have kids form pairs. Hand a piece of string, a paper towel, and two Life Savers candies to each pair, and explain how you performed this trick. Let pairs try the devotion using a paper towel instead of a handkerchief. Encourage kids to present this great devotion to their families and friends. Remind them to tell others that God's love and protection set us free to serve him.

Extra Excitement

● Play a lively outdoor game of Free-Tag. Form two groups, and have each group stand on opposite sides of an imaginary line. (Or you may use jump-ropes laid end-to-end as a center line.) Place a paper cup or beanbag at opposite ends of the playing area. The object is for each group to try and snatch its opponent's cup without getting tagged. If a player is tagged, that player must sit on the sidelines. A player can only be freed when someone from his or her team tags the person. Continue playing until a cup is successfully snatched and carried back to the other side.

TRICKY TIPS

✻ Fruit-flavored Life Savers candies will work if mint ones aren't available.

✻ Practice, practice, practice to make your presentation (and sleight of hand) smooth!

Dancing Doll

The Gift of Grace

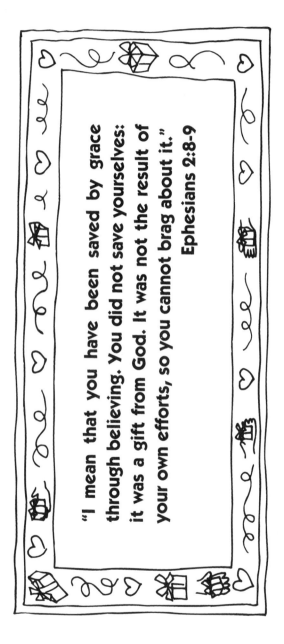

"I mean that you have been saved by grace through believing. You did not save yourselves: it was a gift from God. It was not the result of your own efforts, so you cannot brag about it."
Ephesians 2:8-9

SCRIPTURE INDEX